I0814249

COLLEGE SPORTS ENCYCLOPEDIAS

THE MEN'S COLLEGE BASKETBALL ENCYCLOPEDIA

BY CHARLIE BEATTIE

Encyclopedias

An Imprint of Abdo Reference
abdobooks.com

TABLE OF CONTENTS

10
PURDUE
4
PURDUE
2
BOILERS

THE HISTORY OF MEN'S COLLEGE BASKETBALL

Basketball was invented by Dr. James Naismith in 1891 in Springfield, Massachusetts. Almost immediately, the game spread to college campuses. Within two years, teams were popping up at schools around the country.

Vanderbilt University in Tennessee claims to have played the first college basketball game. A men's team from the school hosted a Nashville YMCA team on February 7, 1893. The first recorded game between two colleges took place in Minnesota on February 9, 1895. Hamline University of Saint Paul hosted Minnesota A&M. The visitors won the game 9–3. By the new century, the game was being played across the country. Even Naismith started a team at the University of Kansas after taking a position there in 1898.

At the time, many people thought sports were improper for women. As a result, college basketball was mostly limited to men for many years. In 1906, the Intercollegiate Athletic Association of the United States (IAAUS) formed. Originally, the organization

James Naismith, who invented basketball, went on to coach the Kansas men's basketball team from 1898 to 1907.

was created to make football safer. But soon it took over the administration of all college sports. In 1910, the IAAUS changed its name to the National Collegiate Athletic Association (NCAA). It's still the biggest organizer of college sports.

Tippy Dye played basketball, baseball, and football at Ohio State during the 1930s. He later became a basketball coach and athletic director at Ohio State and other schools.

Northwestern (in white) and Wisconsin square off in a Big Ten game in 1943. The conference is the oldest in college basketball.

At the time, college basketball was becoming more organized. The Western Conference, which is now called the Big Ten, started in 1896. By 1920, several other conferences had been formed, including early versions of the Southeastern Conference (SEC), Pac-12 Conference, and Big 12 Conference.

TOURNEY TIME

The first attempt to create a men's national championship tournament was in 1922. Six conference champions met in Indianapolis, Indiana, for the three-day National Intercollegiate

Basketball Tournament (NIBT). Wabash College of Indiana defeated Michigan's Kalamazoo College 43–23 in the championship game.

The NIBT lasted only one year, and no other postseason tournament was held for more than a decade. But in the late 1930s, two tournaments were created. Both considered themselves the true championship of college basketball.

The first was the National Invitation Tournament (NIT). Created in 1938 by a group of sportswriters in New York City,

Bob Doll of Colorado goes up for a rebound against Duquesne in a 1940 NIT game.

the NIT held its championship at New York's Madison Square Garden each year. Temple defeated Colorado 60–36 to capture the first title. A year later, the NCAA put together its own tournament. The championship game took place in Evanston, Illinois, with Oregon defeating Ohio State 46–33 to claim the first NCAA title.

The NCAA Tournament was designed to feature the champions of each conference. But in its early years, many teams chose to play in the NIT instead. The NIT was seen as the better tournament. Since the tournament was played in New York, it was much more visible.

Superstar center George Mikan, *left*, led DePaul to the NIT championship in 1945.

BLUE BLOODS

In the 1950s, the NCAA made it mandatory for the biggest conference champions to play in its tournament. By the end of the decade, it had passed the NIT in terms of prestige. While both tournaments are still played today, the NIT field is filled with teams that were left out of the NCAA Tournament.

DOUBLE TITLE WINNER

In the early days of the NCAA Tournament and NIT, it was possible to play in both events. City College of New York became the only school to win both in the same year. The Beavers took both titles in 1950. Starting in 1953, an NCAA rule stated teams could play in only one tournament.

No matter which tournament they played in, several traditional basketball powers claimed their first championships in the 1940s and 1950s. Indiana won its first NCAA title in 1940.

San Francisco teammates carry star center Bill Russell off the floor after the Dons won the 1955 NCAA championship.

Texas Western guard Bobby Joe Hill drives against Kentucky in the 1966 NCAA title game.

The Hoosiers won again in 1953. By then, coach Adolph Rupp's Kentucky Wildcats had won three NCAA championships in four years from 1948 to 1951. Both Kansas and North Carolina won their first NCAA crowns in the 1950s as well.

CHANGING THE GAME

By the start of the 1960s, college basketball had grown in popularity. But the sport still had one huge problem. Black players struggled to find opportunities on top teams. Many Southern schools didn't recruit Black stars at all. Other coaches had an unwritten rule never to have more than three Black players on the court at one time.

Two teams helped bring about change. George Ireland coached Loyola of Illinois. In 1963, he started four Black players in the NCAA championship game against Cincinnati. It was seen as a shocking move. But the Ramblers won the title 60–58.

Three years later, Texas Western started five Black players in the NCAA final against Rupp's all-white Kentucky team. Texas Western, now known as the

NO DUNKS ALLOWED

Starting in 1967, the NCAA banned the slam dunk in college basketball. The organization said that the play was a safety concern. However, many people felt the rule was designed to limit dominant 7-foot, 2-inch UCLA center Lew Alcindor (later known as Kareem Abdul-Jabbar). Critics even named the rule after him. The dunk was banned for nine years before the NCAA overturned the rule.

UCLA coach John Wooden, *left*, and star forward Sidney Wicks hold up the national championship trophy after the Bruins beat Villanova in the 1971 title game.

University of Texas–El Paso (UTEP), won the game 72–65. Though some coaches were slow to integrate their teams, gradually college basketball became a more racially inclusive sport.

THE BIG DANCE

Texas Western's win in 1966 was one of the few in that era not won by the University of California, Los Angeles (UCLA). Coach John Wooden's dominant Bruins captured ten titles in 12 years from 1964 to 1975. It's still the most dominant stretch in the sport's history.

By the end of that run, the NCAA Tournament was growing. In 1974, the tournament included 16 conference champions and nine independent teams. For competitive conferences, that often meant one or more great teams had to stay home.

That became less of a problem when the tournament expanded. It grew to 32 teams in 1975, and then it kept growing to eventually reach 64 teams in 1985.

Though many of the teams in the field were runners-up in bigger conferences, the expanded tournament also included the champions from many smaller leagues around the country. Outside the tournament, those teams rarely had a chance to test themselves against the nation's elite teams. But upsets soon became one of the special charms of the

Players on the Siena College bench celebrate during the team's 80–78 upset over Stanford in the opening round of the 1989 NCAA Tournament.

64-team field. Most years, one or more underdog teams made a deep run. The unpredictability of the tournament led to its "March Madness" nickname.

The NCAA also adopted new rules in the 1980s to make games more exciting. The shot clock was introduced in 1985–86 in an attempt to speed up play. A year later, the NCAA installed a three-point line.

ONE AND DONE

By the 1990s, college basketball's biggest problem was keeping star players in school. By then, the National Basketball Association (NBA) was big business, which meant its players could be paid a lot of money. College players, on the other hand, were forbidden from earning money. As a result, many college stars left early. Some players skipped college and went straight to the NBA.

To combat this, the NBA and NCAA instituted a rule in 2005

Point guard Stephen Curry led little-known Davidson to the Elite Eight of the 2008 NCAA Tournament.

stating players were not eligible until they were a year removed from high school. This resulted in many great players going to college for just that one required year. While some coaches were frustrated by the number of "one-and-done" players in the college game, other coaches embraced it. They took in

Kentucky coach John Calipari, *left*, guided a team filled with freshman stars such as forward Anthony Davis to the 2012 national title.

BUSTED BRACKETS

As the NCAA Tournament expanded, so did fans' interest in trying to predict a winner. In 2023, *Sports Illustrated* magazine estimated that fans filled out anywhere from 60 to 100 million brackets, trying to pick each game's outcome correctly. However, there has never been a recorded perfect bracket. Research shows that the odds of a knowledgeable basketball fan picking every game correctly are around one in 120 billion.

top recruits, hoping to build teams of superstar freshmen. Once those freshmen left, they simply reloaded with a new class of young stars.

BIG MONEY

In 2011, the NCAA Tournament grew to 68 teams. It turned huge profits for the NCAA. But college players were growing frustrated by some of the rules they had to play by. For example, coaches frequently switched jobs, but players who switched schools had to sit out an entire season. Meanwhile, as the sport brought in greater amounts of money, people warmed to the idea of allowing the players to get some of it.

After complaints and lawsuits from players, the NCAA made two huge changes in the 2020s. In 2021, players earned the right to make money off their name, image, and likeness (NIL). Soon, top college players were able to make millions of dollars while still playing college basketball.

Three years later, the NCAA ended its transfer rule. Players were now free to switch schools without missing an entire season. College coaches scrambled to reassemble their

Connecticut (in white) and San Diego State tip off to begin the 2023 NCAA title game.

rosters each year as record numbers of players transferred between seasons.

Schools were also making big changes. For decades, college sports had been organized into regional conferences. That began to change as schools switched their affiliations in order to make more money from television. Some conferences, such as the Big Ten, now stretched across the country. Others, like the Pac-12, were dissolved as teams left.

These changes gave schools and players more freedom. But many fans felt the changes were hurting the game, especially on the men's side. In 2024, the NCAA Tournament lost viewership for the first time in many years. That year, more fans watched the women's final than the men's championship for the first time in the sport's history. Nonetheless, millions of fans continue to tune in when the college basketball season tips off each year.

ALABAMA CRIMSON TIDE

Alabama forward Levi Randolph goes up for a layup in a 2015 game at Coleman Coliseum.

Alabama's men's basketball team has often lived in the shadow of the school's powerful football team. But the Crimson Tide have a proud history on the court as well. The program first tasted success under coach Hank Crisp in the 1920s. In 1929–30, Crisp's team finished 20–0. There was no postseason play at the time. However, a retroactive poll later recognized that Alabama team as the national champion.

Alabama made its debut in the Associated Press (AP) poll in the 1950s. The Tide were ranked twelfth at the end of the 1954–55 season. The next year, a team nicknamed "The Rocket 8" reached as high as fourth. Alabama's star was forward Jerry Harper, who scored more than 1,800 points in his career.

Coach C. M. Newton took the Crimson Tide to the NCAA Tournament for the first time in 1975. That team lost in the first round of the 32-team tournament. A year later, powerful center Leon Douglas led Alabama to its first tournament win, a 79–64

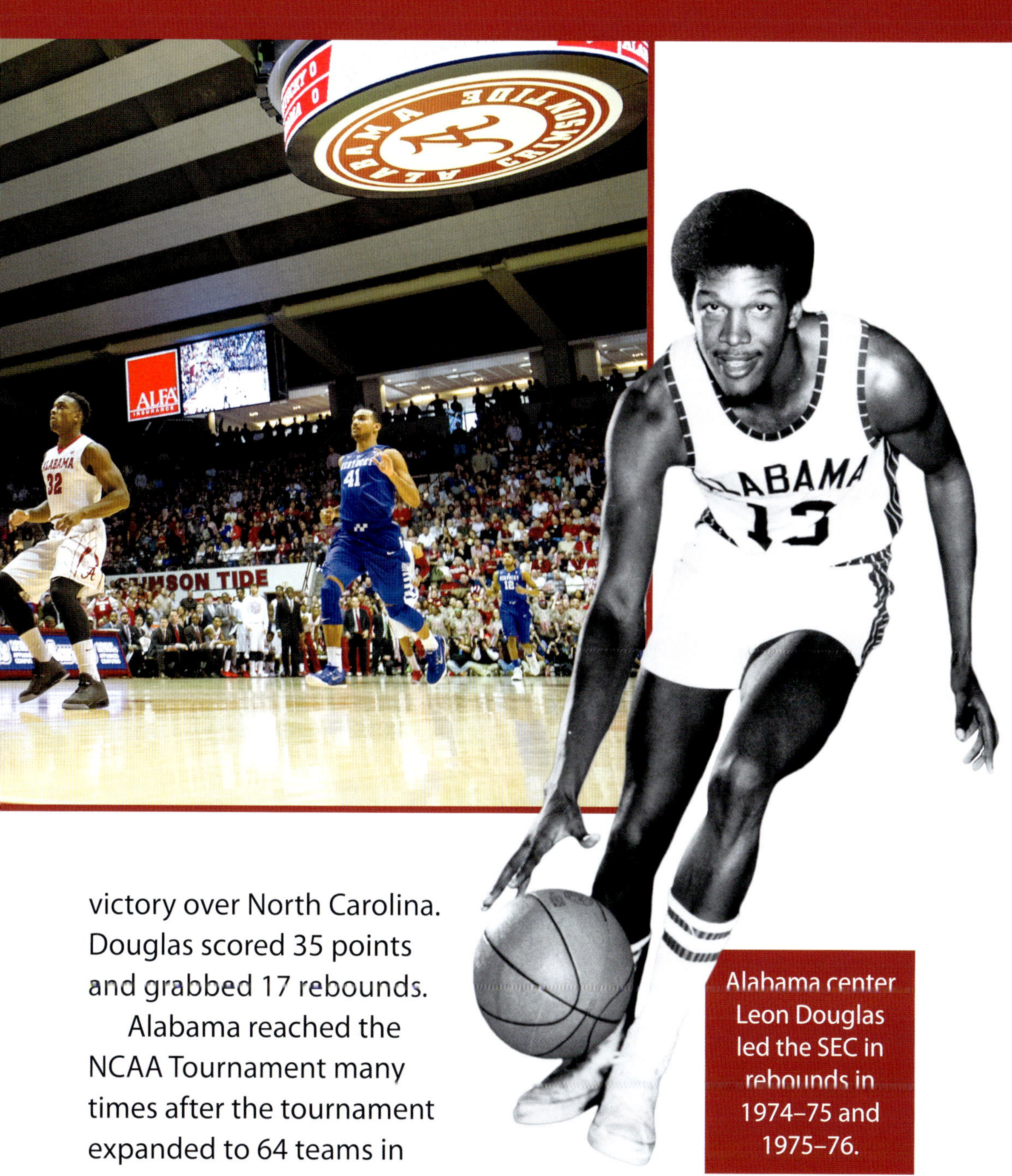

victory over North Carolina. Douglas scored 35 points and grabbed 17 rebounds.

Alabama reached the NCAA Tournament many times after the tournament expanded to 64 teams in the 1980s. But most of the Tide's

Alabama center Leon Douglas led the SEC in rebounds in 1974–75 and 1975–76.

Alabama coach Nate Oats holds up the regional championship trophy after Alabama beat Clemson in the 2024 Elite Eight.

THE PLAID PALACE

Wimp Sanderson was Alabama's coach from 1981 to 1992. Sanderson was known for wearing colorful plaid sport coats during games. In his honor, Alabama painted its center-court logo in a plaid pattern. Ever since, Coleman Coliseum has been known as "The Plaid Palace."

runs ended early. Coach Mark Gottfried guided Alabama to its first Elite Eight in 2004 before losing to eventual champion Connecticut.

Two decades later, coach Nate Oats led the nation's highest-scoring team into the tournament. After a narrow 89–87 win over No. 1 seed North Carolina in the Sweet 16, Alabama faced Clemson in the Elite Eight. Behind 54 second-half points, the Tide reached their first Final Four with an 89–82 win. Alabama then lost to Connecticut in the national semifinals 86–72.

FACT BOX

First Season: 1912–13

Location: Tuscaloosa, Alabama

Arena: Coleman Coliseum

Conference: Southeastern Conference

All-Time Record: 1,820–1,108–1

NCAA Tournament Appearances: 25

Final Fours: 1

National Titles: None

Top Coaches: C. M. Newton (1969–80); Mark Gottfried (1999–2009); Nate Oats (2020–)

Top Players: Jerry Harper (1952–56); Leon Douglas (1972–76); T. R. Dunn (1973–77); Reggie King (1975–79); Eddie Phillips (1978–82); Robert Horry (1988–92); James Robinson (1990–93); Trevor Releford (2010–14)

Mascot: Big Al

ARIZONA WILDCATS

Arizona's basketball program was founded in 1904. Two coaches have played huge roles in the team's history. Fred Enke took over in 1925 and led Arizona for 35 seasons. Later, Lute Olson coached the Wildcats from 1983 to 2007.

Arizona enjoyed mostly winning seasons under Enke, and he led the Wildcats to their first NCAA Tournament in 1951. But between Enke's retirement in 1961 and the hiring of Olson

Coach Lute Olson had a record of 587–190 over 24 seasons at Arizona.

22 years later, Arizona made it to the tournament only twice. When Olson took over in 1983, the Wildcats were coming off four straight losing seasons. After going 11–17 his first year, Olson never again finished under .500.

The Wildcats reached the No. 1 spot in the AP poll for the first time in 1987–88. Behind forward Sean Elliott, Arizona's all-time leading scorer, the team went 35–3 and reached the Final Four. It was the first of 20 consecutive 20-win seasons for Olson.

The Wildcats went back to the Final Four in 1994. Three years later, the 25–10 Wildcats entered the tournament as a No. 4 seed. Then Arizona knocked off tournament favorite Kansas in

Forward Sean Elliott was a two-time All-American in his four seasons at Arizona in the late 1980s.

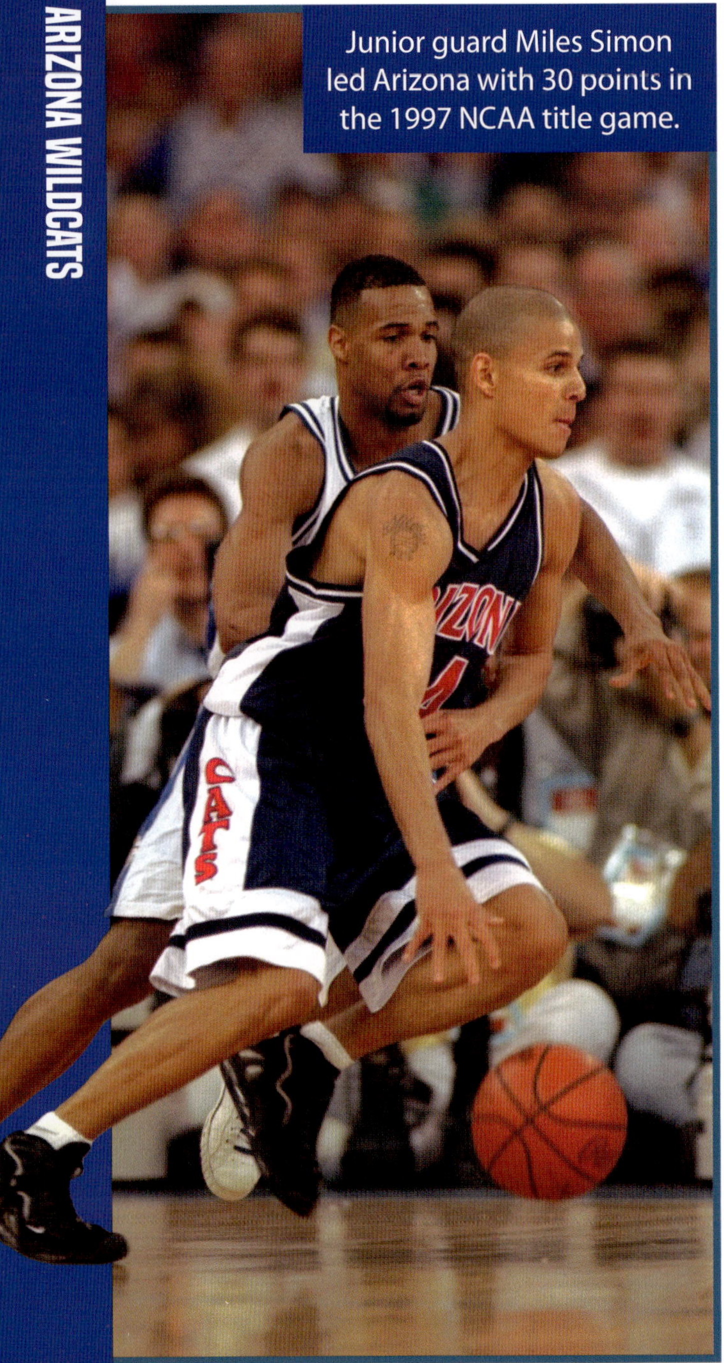

Junior guard Miles Simon led Arizona with 30 points in the 1997 NCAA title game.

the Sweet 16. The Wildcats downed another top seed, North Carolina, in the national semifinals. That set up a matchup with a third No. 1 seed, Kentucky, in the championship game.

With guards Mike Bibby and Miles Simon leading the way for Arizona, the two teams battled to a 74–74 tie at the end of regulation. Arizona didn't hit a single shot from the floor in overtime, but the team hit ten free throws to pull out an 84–79 victory. Arizona became the first team ever to beat three No. 1 seeds on its way to a championship.

Olson took Arizona to the title game

again in 2001. He then got the team back to a pair of Elite Eights before stepping down in 2007. The Wildcats' 25-year streak of NCAA Tournament appearances ended in 2010. Coach Sean Miller recovered to post four 30-win seasons before leaving the program in 2021.

PLAYING FOR BOBBI

Lute Olson's wife, Bobbi, was a very active figure in Arizona's basketball program. When Bobbi passed away before the 2001 NCAA Tournament, the players dedicated their performance to her. Arizona nearly won the national championship. The Wildcats fell to Duke 82–72 in the title game.

FACT BOX

First Season: 1904–05

Location: Tucson, Arizona

Arena: McKale Center

Conference: Big 12 Conference

All-Time Record: 1,913–999–1

NCAA Tournament Appearances: 34

Final Fours: 4

National Titles: 1997

Top Coaches: Fred Enke (1925–61); Lute Olson (1983–2007); Sean Miller (2009–21)

Top Players: Sean Elliott (1985–89); Khalid Reeves (1990–94); Damon Stoudamire (1991–95); Miles Simon (1994–98); Mike Bibby (1996–98); Jason Terry (1995–99); Jason Gardner (1999–2003); Channing Frye (2001–05)

Mascot: Wilbur and Wilma Wildcat

ARKANSAS RAZORBACKS

Arkansas guard Sidney Moncrief, *right*, goes up for a layup against Kentucky in the 1978 Final Four.

The Arkansas Razorbacks have a long history of success in both the SEC and the NCAA Tournament. Arkansas won its first NCAA Tournament game in 1941. After finishing 19–2 in the regular season, coach Glen Rose's team knocked off Wyoming 52–40 in the first round of the eight-team tournament. The Razorbacks then lost to Washington State in the Final Four.

Coach Eddie Sutton took Arkansas back to the Final Four of the 32-team NCAA Tournament in 1978. Sutton's team was led by "The Triplets." Athletic guards Ron Brewer and Sidney Moncrief and forward Marvin Delph were all Arkansas natives. They led the Razorbacks to a 32–4 record. Arkansas knocked off powerhouse UCLA before losing to rival Kentucky 64–59 in the Final Four. The Razorbacks beat Notre Dame 71–69 in the third-place game.

Sutton coached the Razorbacks until 1985. He was then replaced by Nolan Richardson. The fiery Richardson liked up-tempo basketball and played a swarming defensive style. He worked his players hard in the offseason to build up their stamina. That way they could chase opposing offenses all over the court. Richardson called his style "Hog Ball."

Led by the school's all-time leading scorer, Todd Day, Arkansas got back to the Final Four in 1990. Richardson then

Forward Corliss Williamson led Arkansas with 23 points in the 1994 NCAA championship game.

FAN IN CHIEF

Former Arkansas governor Bill Clinton was president during the Razorbacks' championship run in 1994. Clinton was a big fan of the team. He attended multiple NCAA Tournament games. The commander in chief even celebrated on the court with Nolan Richardson after the Razorbacks' championship-game victory.

led the Razorbacks on a thrilling run to the championship game against Duke in 1994. Arkansas fell behind by 10 points early in the second half. But the Razorbacks turned up the tempo and made a quick comeback. With 51 seconds left, guard Scotty Thurman hit a contested three-point

Coach Nolan Richardson holds up the national championship trophy after the Razorbacks' victory over Duke in the 1994 NCAA final.

shot to break a 70–70 tie. Arkansas held on to win 76–72 for the school's first title. The Razorbacks went back to the championship game in 1995. However, this time they lost to UCLA.

The school fired Richardson in 2002 after a salary dispute. Several coaches have tried to get Arkansas back to the top. Eric Musselman took the Razorbacks to consecutive Elite Eight appearances in 2021 and 2022. Before the 2024–25 season, Arkansas hired big-name coach John Calipari away from Kentucky in hopes of getting over the hump.

FACT BOX

First Season: 1923–24

Location: Fayetteville, Arkansas

Arena: Bud Walton Arena

Conference: Southeastern Conference

All-Time Record: 1,832–1,008

NCAA Tournament Appearances: 37

Final Fours: 6

National Titles: 1994

Top Coaches: Glen Rose (1933–42, 1952–66); Eddie Sutton (1974–85); Nolan Richardson (1985–2002)

Top Players: George Kok (1944–48); Ron Brewer (1975–78); Sidney Moncrief (1975–79); Scott Hastings (1978–82); Lee Mayberry (1988–92); Todd Day (1988–92); Corliss Williamson (1992–95); Bobby Portis (2013–15)

Mascot: Tusk, Big Red, Sue E, Pork Chop

AUBURN TIGERS

Auburn doesn't have the consistent history of some of its SEC rivals. But the Tigers have enjoyed some electrifying moments on the basketball court. In 1958 and 1959, Auburn put together a 30-game winning streak. The run was led by powerful rebounder Rex Frederick and All-America guard Henry Hart. During the 1958–59 season, coach Joel Eaves's team reached as high as No. 2 in the AP poll.

Auburn players celebrate with coach Bruce Pearl after beating Michigan in the Sweet 16 of the 2025 NCAA Tournament.

Auburn center Charles Barkley looks to pass in a 1984 game against Vanderbilt. Barkley went on to a Hall of Fame career.

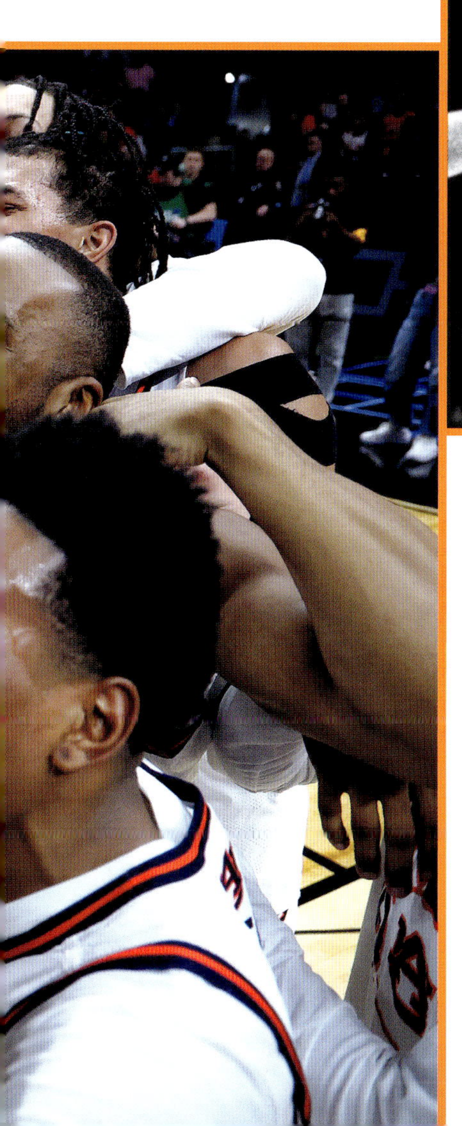

Frederick and Hart never played in the NCAA Tournament. Auburn didn't reach the tournament until 1984, after the field had been expanded to 53 teams. Two years later, Auburn's all-time leading scorer Chuck Person led the Tigers on a Cinderella run. Auburn entered the field as a No. 8 seed. But the Tigers upset top-seeded Saint John's in the second round behind Person's 27 points and 15 rebounds. Auburn reached the Elite Eight before losing to eventual champion Louisville.

Tigers fans had to wait 33 years to make a deeper run in the tournament. Coach Bruce Pearl's team made the 2019 tournament as a No. 5 seed. In the Elite Eight, guards Jared Harper and Bryce Brown combined to score 50 points as the Tigers outlasted No. 2 seed Kentucky 77–71 in overtime. The win put Auburn in the Final Four for the first time.

Facing tournament favorite Virginia, Auburn rallied from 10 points down to lead 62–60 with seconds to go. Virginia's Kyle Guy had a chance to win the game with a three-pointer at the buzzer, but his shot missed. Auburn's players erupted

Auburn guard Bryce Brown goes up for a last-second shot against Virginia in the 2019 Final Four.

THE TELEGRAM TRAIL

Auburn put its 30-game winning streak on the line in February 1959 with a trip to powerhouse Kentucky. With the Tigers on the road, a member of the school's spirit committee organized a plan to have more than 8,000 telegrams sent to the team. Telegrams were notes sent electronically and then printed out at the new location. Despite all the notes of support, Auburn lost 75–56 and the streak ended.

in celebration before realizing an official had called a shooting foul on the Tigers. Guy sank all three free throws with 0.6 seconds left to end Auburn's run.

Pearl led the Tigers back to the Final Four in 2025. But once again the run ended in heartbreaking fashion. Auburn led conference-rival Florida by nine points early in the second half, but the Tigers struggled to score down the stretch and fell 79–73.

FACT BOX

First Season: 1905–06

Location: Auburn, Alabama

Arena: Neville Arena

Conference: Southeastern Conference

All-Time Record: 1,498–1,256–1

NCAA Tournament Appearances: 14

Final Fours: 2

National Titles: None

Top Coaches: Joel Eaves (1949–63); Cliff Ellis (1994–2004); Bruce Pearl (2014–)

Top Players: Rex Frederick (1956–59); John Mengelt (1968–71); Mike Mitchell (1974–78); Charles Barkley (1981–84); Chuck Person (1982–86); Wesley Person (1990–94); Chris Porter (1998–2000); Johni Broome (2022–25)

Mascot: Aubie the Tiger

Baylor first emerged as a basketball power just one year after a winless season. In 1944–45, the Bears finished the season 0–17. New coach Bill Henderson then led Baylor to a 25–5 record in his first year. The Bears were eliminated in their first NCAA Tournament game. But two years later, they reached the title game. There they lost 58–42 to Kentucky.

The Bears reached the NCAA Tournament again in 1950. But then the team went into a long dry spell. For the rest of the 1900s, Baylor reached the NCAA Tournament only once and did not win a game.

Things got worse in 2003. A series of scandals, including the murder of a player by a teammate, nearly destroyed the school's basketball program. The school hired energetic coach Scott Drew in 2003. He needed to clean up Baylor basketball's image both on and off the court.

Baylor opened a new arena, Foster Pavilion, in January 2024.

Though he took over a team that was on probation through 2010, Drew soon made Baylor a winner. Focusing on unselfish team play, Drew led the Bears back to the NCAA Tournament in 2008. In 2010, the program's all-time leading scorer, LaceDarius Dunn, led Baylor to the Elite Eight. The Bears again fell one step short of the Final Four in 2012.

In 2020–21, Drew led Baylor to its fourteenth straight winning season at 22–2. The Bears then rolled through the NCAA Tournament. They reached the final against undefeated Gonzaga. Led by 22 points from guard Jared Butler and stingy defense, Baylor finished off their championship season with an 86–70 victory.

Guard LaceDarius Dunn finished his Baylor career in 2011 with 2,285 points.

Baylor coach Scott Drew holds up a piece of the net after the Bears beat Gonzaga for the 2021 NCAA championship.

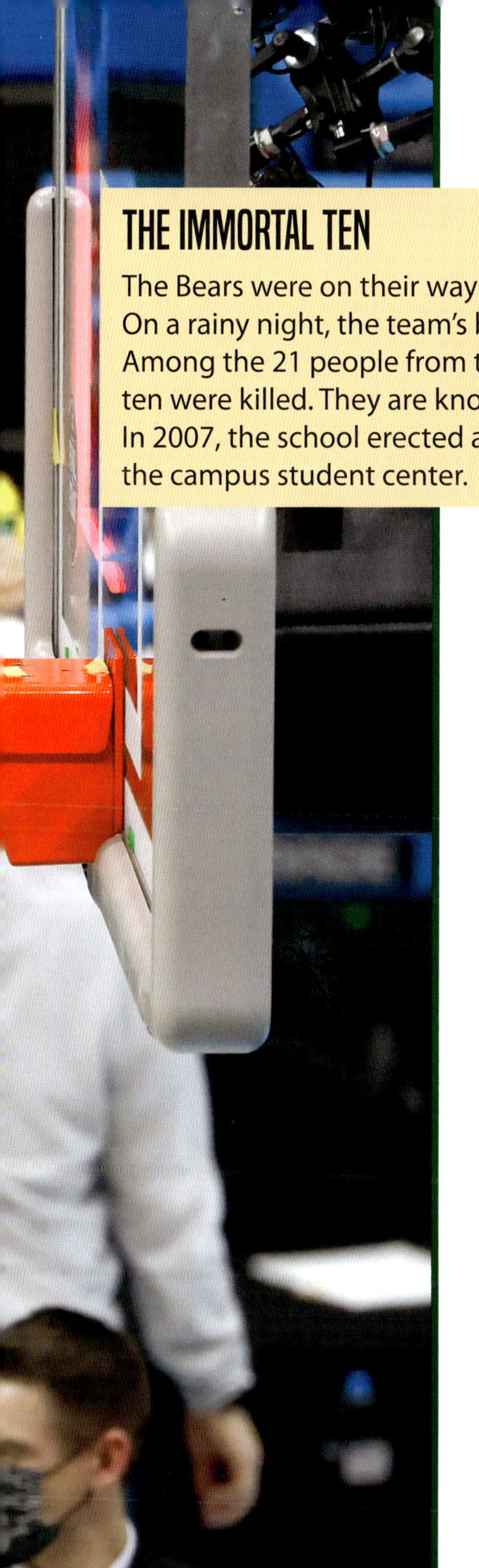

THE IMMORTAL TEN

The Bears were on their way to play Texas on January 22, 1927. On a rainy night, the team's bus was hit by an oncoming train. Among the 21 people from the Baylor party on board the bus, ten were killed. They are known at Baylor as "The Immortal Ten." In 2007, the school erected a statue of the Immortal Ten outside the campus student center.

FACT BOX

First Season: 1906–07

Location: Waco, Texas

Arena: Foster Pavilion

Conference: Big 12 Conference

All-Time Record: 1,499–1,423

NCAA Tournament Appearances: 17

Final Fours: 3

National Titles: 2021

Top Coaches: Ralph Wolf (1926–41); Bill Henderson (1941–43, 1945–61); Scott Drew (2003–)

Top Players: Don Heathington (1947–50); Vinnie Johnson (1977–79); Terry Teagle (1978–82); Micheal Williams (1984–88); Brian Skinner (1994–98); Curtis Jerrells (2005–09); LaceDarius Dunn (2007–11); Jared Butler (2018–21)

Mascot: Bruiser and Marigold

CINCINNATI BEARCATS

Cincinnati was one of the premier basketball programs in the 1950s and early 1960s. Under coach George Smith, the Bearcats began a streak of reaching every Final Four from

Cincinnati guard Oscar Robertson (12) averaged 33.8 points per game from 1957 to 1960. He led the nation in scoring in each of his three seasons with the Bearcats.

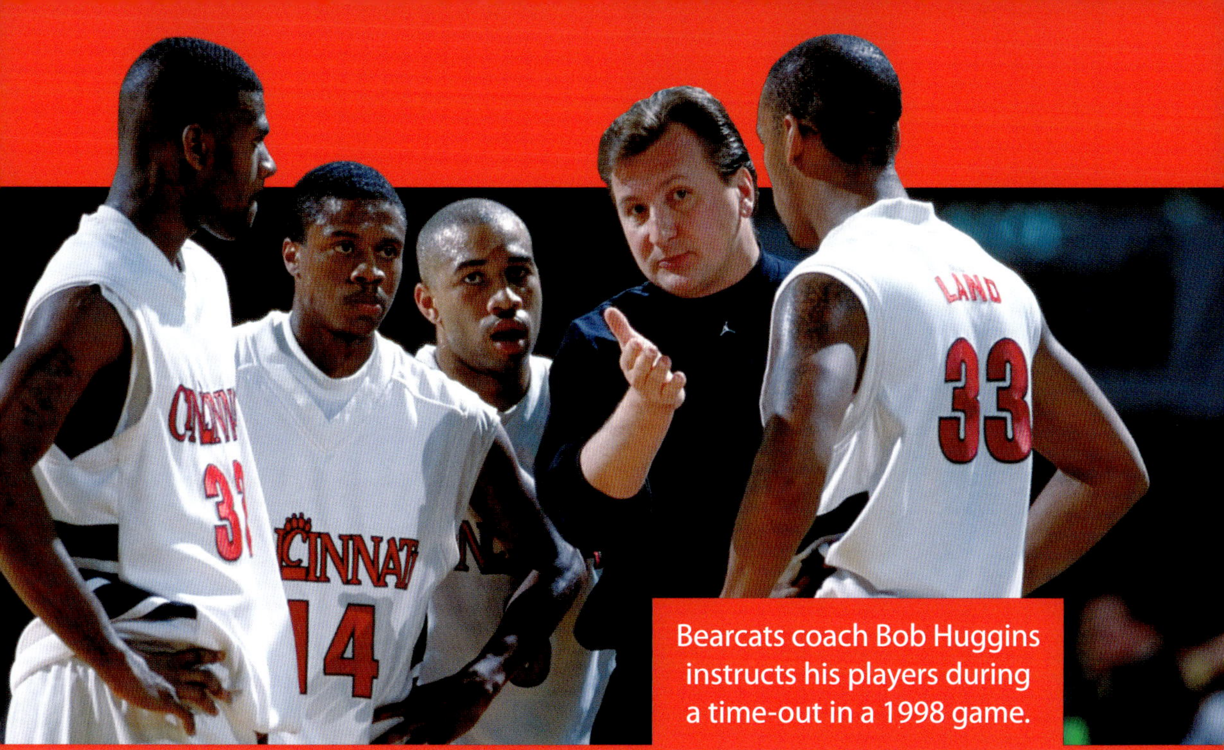
Bearcats coach Bob Huggins instructs his players during a time-out in a 1998 game.

1959 to 1963. The 1959 team was led by electrifying junior guard Oscar Robertson, who averaged 32.6 points per game. Robertson led Cincinnati back to the Final Four a year later by averaging 33.7 points per contest. However, in both years the Bearcats were beaten in the national semifinals.

Robertson left for the NBA before the 1960–61 season, and Smith became the school's athletic director. But new coach Ed Jucker still had an excellent frontcourt. Center Paul Hogue and forwards Tom Thacker and Bob Wiesenhahn led Cincinnati to a 23–3 regular-season record. The Bearcats then outlasted defending champion Ohio State 70–65 in overtime to capture the national title.

Jucker's Bearcats finished 25–2 in 1961–62. In the national semifinals, Cincinnati rallied to beat UCLA 72–70 on a last-second shot by Thacker. It was the forward's only basket of the game. That set up a championship rematch with Ohio State.

THE CROSSTOWN SHOOTOUT

Cincinnati shares a heated rivalry with Xavier. The two schools are just 2 miles (3.2 km) apart. The game has become known as "The Crosstown Shootout." In 1990, the game was being played at the same time as President George H. W. Bush's State of the Union address. The local TV station broadcasting the game refused to cut away to show the president's speech.

Hogue led the way with 22 points and 19 rebounds as the Bearcats won 71–59.

Jucker took Cincinnati to its fifth straight Final Four in 1963. But after that, the Bearcats reached the

Cincinnati guard Sean Kilpatrick goes up for a jump shot against rival Xavier in 2012. Kilpatrick finished his Bearcats career with 2,145 points, second only to Oscar Robertson.

tournament only four times between 1964 and 1991. Things got better soon after demanding coach Bob Huggins took over in 1989. He led the Bearcats to the NCAA Tournament in 1992 as a No. 4 seed. Cincinnati then went on a run that ended only in the Final Four against Michigan. It was the first of 14 straight tournament appearances for the Bearcats under Huggins.

Huggins left the program in 2005. Coach Mick Cronin took over a year later. After a few down years, Cronin began a new streak of nine tournament appearances between 2011 and 2019 before leaving Cincinnati for UCLA.

FACT BOX

First Season: 1901–02

Location: Cincinnati, Ohio

Arena: Fifth Third Arena

Conference: Big 12 Conference

All-Time Record: 1,930–1,095

NCAA Tournament Appearances: 33

Final Fours: 6

National Titles: 1961, 1962

Top Coaches: Ed Jucker (1960–65); Bob Huggins (1989–2005); Mick Cronin (2006–19)

Top Players: Jack Twyman (1951–55); Oscar Robertson (1957–60); Tom Thacker (1960–63); Lloyd Batts (1971–74); Danny Fortson (1994–97); Kenyon Martin (1996–2000); Steve Logan (1998–2002); Sean Kilpatrick (2010–14)

Mascot: The Bearcat

Connecticut was a successful program in the 1950s and 1960s while playing in the Yankee Conference. The Huskies won the small conference 22 times between 1925 and 1970. But the team better known as UConn ran into trouble when it joined the powerful Big East in 1979.

After four losing seasons, the Huskies hired Jim Calhoun as coach in 1986. By 1990, Calhoun's team featured the program's all-time leading scorer Chris Smith at guard. Behind him, UConn reached the Elite Eight.

With a cast of new stars such as sharpshooting guard Ray Allen, Calhoun and the Huskies kept rising. Finally, in 1999,

Coach Jim Calhoun had a 625–243 all-time record at Connecticut from 1986 to 2012.

UConn broke through. Behind the backcourt of Khalid El-Amin and Richard "Rip" Hamilton, the Huskies finished 34–2. UConn finished the year by topping powerhouse Duke 77–74 in the NCAA title game. Hamilton led the way with 27 points.

Calhoun took a new group back to the championship in 2004. This time, the combination of accurate shooting guard Ben Gordon and powerful center Emeka Okafor guided UConn. The Huskies rallied to beat Duke 79–78 in the Final Four. They then held off Georgia Tech 82–73 in the championship game.

The Huskies made it back to the Final Four twice more under Calhoun. They lost in the semifinals in 2009. In 2011, high-scoring

UConn guard Kemba Walker holds up the national championship trophy after the Huskies' victory in 2011.

guard Kemba Walker led UConn on a surprise run. The No. 3–seeded Huskies smothered Butler 53–41 in the title game. Calhoun retired after the next season.

Former UConn player Kevin Ollie took over as head coach. In 2014, he led the team on another Cinderella NCAA Tournament run. The Huskies entered the tournament as a No. 7 seed. Senior guard Shabazz Napier scored 22 points in the championship game as UConn beat Kentucky 60–54.

Ollie left UConn in 2018 after committing recruiting violations. New coach Dan Hurley overcame two years of probation to get UConn back on top in 2023. The Huskies won every NCAA Tournament game by double figures. They finished the tournament by routing San Diego State 76–59. Hurley's team then breezed to another title the next year. The Huskies outscored their six tournament opponents by a record 23.3 points per game. Though UConn became a power only in the 1990s, the team's sixth title gave it more national championships than every team except for UCLA, Kentucky, and North Carolina.

WALKER'S WINNERS

To win the ultra-competitive Big East Conference tournament in 2011, UConn needed to win five games in five days. Kemba Walker put in a star performance. He hit a game-winning shot at the buzzer to beat Pittsburgh in the quarterfinals. He then scored 33 points in the semis and 19 more in the championship game. Walker totaled 130 points in the five victories. That broke the old tournament record by 46 points.

Connecticut guard Hassan Diarra goes up for a layup in the Huskies' 75–60 victory over Purdue in the 2024 NCAA title game.

FACT BOX

First Season: 1900–01

Location: Storrs, Connecticut

Arena: Gampel Pavilion; XL Center

Conference: Big East Conference

All-Time Record: 1,861–1,026

NCAA Tournament Appearances: 37

Final Fours: 7

National Titles: 1999, 2004, 2011, 2014, 2023, 2024

Top Coaches: Hugh Greer (1946–63); Jim Calhoun (1986–2012); Dan Hurley (2018–)

Top Players: Tony Hanson (1973–77); Chris Smith (1988–92); Ray Allen (1993–96); Richard Hamilton (1996–99); Emeka Okafor (2001–04); Kemba Walker (2008–11); Shabazz Napier (2010–14); Tristen Newton (2022–24)

Mascot: Jonathan the Husky

DUKE BLUE DEVILS

Duke forward Cooper Flagg backs down a North Carolina defender in a 2025 rivalry game between the two schools.

Few college men's basketball programs are as well-known as Duke. The Blue Devils share one of the sport's fiercest rivalries with neighboring North Carolina. The schools helped found the highly regarded Atlantic Coast Conference (ACC) in 1953. In most seasons, the neighbors battle for the league's regular-season and tournament titles.

Duke reached the Final Four three times in the 1960s playing coach Vic Bubas's up-tempo style. The Blue Devils got all the way to the championship game in 1978 under coach Bill Foster. But all four times, they came up short.

After Foster left in 1980, Duke hired little-known 33-year-old Mike Krzyzewski. In his first few seasons, "Coach K" struggled while North Carolina and North Carolina State each won national titles. Many Duke fans

Duke's Mike Krzyzewski was the first NCAA men's coach to reach 1,000 victories. He retired in 2022 with 1,129 wins.

THE CAMERON CRAZIES

Duke's Cameron Indoor Stadium is a small venue. The school's student section is very close to the court. Over the years, Duke's students have developed an intimidating atmosphere for opponents. Many cover themselves in blue and white paint. They also creatively taunt opposing players for missed shots and turnovers. The student section is known as "The Cameron Crazies."

JJ Redick set Duke's scoring record with 2,769 points between 2002 and 2006.

wanted the young coach fired. The Blue Devils stuck with him, and Krzyzewski delivered seven Final Fours in nine seasons between 1986 and 1994.

Led by guard Bobby Hurley, forward Grant Hill, and center Christian Laettner, Duke broke through in 1991. The Blue Devils knocked off Kansas 72–65 in the championship game. Duke won a second straight title in 1992 by beating Michigan 71–51.

By the time Duke won another title in 2001, the Blue Devils were one of the most envied programs in college basketball. Year after year, Krzyzewski brought in top recruiting classes. His teams won at least 30 games in 16 different seasons. In 2010, the Blue Devils won a fourth title when they outlasted Butler 61–59 in the championship game. Krzyzewski added a fifth championship in 2015. The Blue Devils rallied to beat Wisconsin 68–63 and cap a 35–4 season.

FACT BOX

First Season: 1905–06

Location: Durham, North Carolina

Arena: Cameron Indoor Stadium

Conference: Atlantic Coast Conference

All-Time Record: 2,335–933

NCAA Tournament Appearances: 47

Final Fours: 18

National Titles: 1991, 1992, 2001, 2010, 2015

Top Coaches: Vic Bubas (1959–69); Bill Foster (1974–80); Mike Krzyzewski (1980–2022)

Top Players: Art Heyman (1960–63); Mike Gminski (1976–80); Johnny Dawkins (1982–86); Christian Laettner (1988–92); Bobby Hurley (1989–93); Grant Hill (1990–94); Shane Battier (1997–2001); JJ Redick (2002–06)

Mascot: The Blue Devil

When Krzyzewski retired after the 2021–22 season, he was the winningest coach in college basketball. Only three schools had more than his five national championships. Krzyzewski also ranked first with 101 wins in the NCAA Tournament.

One of Krzyzewski's former star players, Jon Scheyer, took over as head coach. Scheyer kept the school's strong tradition going. He led Duke to the Final Four in his third season.

Christian Laettner's basket is still regarded as one of the most famous in NCAA Tournament history.

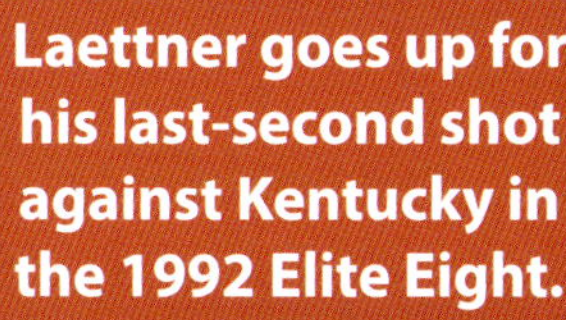

Laettner goes up for his last-second shot against Kentucky in the 1992 Elite Eight.

THE SHOT

Top-seeded Duke trailed No. 2 Kentucky 103–102 with 2.1 seconds left in overtime of the 1992 Elite Eight. Forward Grant Hill threw a long pass to star senior Christian Laettner at the Kentucky free-throw line. With his back to the basket, Laettner faked to his right. He then turned and shot over Kentucky defender Deron Feldhaus. The buzzer-beating basket won the game, and a few days later Duke went on to win its second NCAA title in a row. Laettner's iconic basket became known as "The Shot."

FLORIDA GATORS

Florida's basketball program was founded in 1915, but the team wasn't very well organized. The Gators didn't have a full-time coach until 1960 and didn't reach the NCAA Tournament until 1987. Florida also struggled off the court. When coach Lon Kruger arrived in 1989, the Gators were on probation.

Gators forward Andrew DeClercq, *left*, and guard Dan Cross celebrate a basket during Florida's Final Four run in 1994.

Kruger slowly improved the team. He took a surprising Florida squad to the Final Four in 1994. However, Kruger left two years later to become the coach at Illinois.

Billy Donovan replaced Kruger. After posting losing records in his first two seasons, Donovan took Florida to the Sweet 16 in 1999 and then the national championship game in 2000. The Gators beat blue blood programs Duke and North Carolina before falling to Michigan State in the final.

Donovan kept the momentum going. By 2005–06, he had built a gritty, defense-oriented team. The Gators started the season unranked but reeled off 17 straight wins. After finishing 27–6, Florida advanced to the national final against a storied UCLA program. Led by hard-nosed center Joakim Noah's six blocked shots, the Gators smothered the Bruins 75–57 to win Florida's first title.

A year later, Florida had a chance to become the first back-to-back national champion since Duke in 1991 and 1992. The Gators featured five double-digit scorers. Their team-first approach carried them into the final against Ohio State. There, forward Al Horford

Florida's Al Horford slams home two points in the 2006 NCAA title game against UCLA.

led the way with 18 points in an 84–75 win.

Donovan coached the Gators to another Final Four in 2014. He left a year later as the school's all-time winningest coach. At first, the Gators struggled to replace Donovan. Coach Todd Golden arrived in 2022. After a losing record in his first season, he led rapid rebirth.

Florida finished the 2024–25 season 30–4. Led by high-scoring guard Walter Clayton Jr., the Gators reached the Final Four. After rallying to beat Auburn, the Gators faced Houston in the final. Florida trailed for much of the game. But the Gators held Houston without a point for the last 2:05. With a 65–63 win, Florida claimed its third NCAA title.

BRINGING IT HOME

Florida did more than bring home the national championship trophy from the 2006 Final Four in Indianapolis. The school's athletic department bought the court used for the semifinals and championship games. They installed the floor at Florida's home arena, the O'Connell Center. Florida's teams played on the championship court until 2016. The court was then broken up and sold in pieces as souvenirs.

Guard Walter Clayton Jr. does the Gator Chomp celebration after Florida beat Houston to win the 2025 NCAA title.

FACT BOX

First Season: 1915–16

Location: Gainesville, Florida

Arena: Exactech Arena at the Stephen C. O'Connell Center

Conference: Southeastern Conference

All-Time Record: 1,565–1,190

NCAA Tournament Appearances: 23

Final Fours: 6

National Titles: 2006, 2007, 2025

Top Coaches: Lon Kruger (1990–96); Billy Donovan (1996–2015); Todd Golden (2022–)

Top Players: Neal Walk (1966–69); Ronnie Williams (1980–84); Vernon Maxwell (1984–88); Udonis Haslem (1998–2002); Joakim Noah (2004–07); Corey Brewer (2004–07); Kenny Boynton (2009–13); Chris Chiozza (2014–18)

Mascot: Albert and Alberta Gator

GEORGETOWN HOYAS

Georgetown reached the national title game in 1943. But that was a rare moment of success in the first 70 years of the program. When the Hoyas hired new coach John Thompson Jr. in 1972, the team was coming off a 3–23 season.

The imposing 6-foot-10 Thompson had been a backup center on the Boston Celtics' NBA dynasty teams of the 1950s and 1960s. He quickly brought that winning attitude to the nation's capital. The Hoyas reached the NCAA Tournament for the first time in 32 seasons in 1975. In 1982, Georgetown reached the national title game. However, the Hoyas were beaten 63–62 on a late basket by North Carolina's star freshman, Michael Jordan.

Thompson's teams played smothering, aggressive defense. Many opponents thought the team was too rough. The fear of playing Georgetown became known as "Hoya paranoia."

Coach John Thompson Jr. had a 596–239 record in 27 seasons at Georgetown from 1972 to 1999. The Hoyas reached the NCAA Tournament or NIT in 24 of those seasons.

Center Patrick Ewing had 493 blocked shots in four seasons at Georgetown. He was the No. 1 pick in the 1985 NBA Draft.

Thompson didn't listen to the critics and kept on winning. His team was built around dominant 7-foot, 1-inch center Patrick Ewing. In 1984, Ewing averaged 16.4 points, 10.0 rebounds, and 3.6 blocks per game. The All-American led Georgetown to a 34–3 record. The Hoyas outlasted a high-scoring Houston team 84–75 in the national title game. Ewing blocked four shots and was one of five double-digit scorers for Georgetown. With the win, Thompson became the first Black head coach to lead a national-championship team.

Thompson, Ewing, and Georgetown looked set for a second title in 1985. They faced Big East rival Villanova in the title game. During the regular season, the Hoyas had beaten the Wildcats twice. But Villanova pulled off a shocking 66–64 upset in the championship game.

Georgetown remained strong. Powerful center Alonzo Mourning and electrifying guard Allen Iverson became stars.

Guard Allen Iverson averaged a Georgetown-record 25.0 points per game in 1995–96.

THE KENTE CLOTH

Georgetown's uniforms featured unique patterns in the 1990s. The sides of the uniforms featured a design made to look like West African kente cloth. The real cloth is a handwoven combination of silk and cotton. In West African cultures, it represents wealth and royalty. Hoyas coach John Thompson Jr. worked with Nike to design the pattern.

But Thompson never reached another Final Four. He resigned in 1999.

Five years later, his son, John Thompson III, took over. The younger Thompson led Georgetown back to the Final Four in 2007 but couldn't sustain that success. Thompson III left the team in 2017. In 2021, Ewing coached the Hoyas to their first NCAA Tournament appearance in six years.

FACT BOX

First Season: 1906–07

Location: Washington, DC

Arena: Capital One Arena

Conference: Big East Conference

All-Time Record: 1,740–1,172

NCAA Tournament Appearances: 31

Final Fours: 5

National Titles: 1984

Top Coaches: Elmer Ripley (1927–29, 1938–43, 1946–49); John Thompson Jr. (1972–99); John Thompson III (2004–17)

Top Players: Sleepy Floyd (1978–82); Patrick Ewing (1981–85); David Wingate (1982–86); Reggie Williams (1983–87); Dikembe Mutombo (1988–91); Alonzo Mourning (1988–92); Allen Iverson (1994–96); Roy Hibbert (2004–08); D'Vauntes Smith-Rivera (2012–16)

Mascot: Jack the Bulldog

GONZAGA BULLDOGS

Many college basketball fans didn't know much about Gonzaga when the school entered the 1999 NCAA Tournament as a No. 10 seed. The Bulldogs had been to the tournament only once before. The school from eastern Washington was best known as the alma mater of NBA superstar point guard John Stockton.

The Bulldogs announced themselves with a thrilling run to the Elite Eight under coach Dan Monson. Monson left the program after the season. But Gonzaga

Gonzaga players celebrate after upsetting Florida 73–72 in the 1999 Sweet 16.

Gonzaga forward Adam Morrison led the nation in scoring in 2005–06.

continued its momentum under new coach Mark Few. The Bulldogs reached the Sweet 16 in each of the next two seasons.

As Gonzaga's streak of NCAA Tournament appearances continued, the program became less of an underdog. Under Few, the Bulldogs earned a top-four seed in the NCAA Tournament four times between 2004 and 2009. But winning in the tournament proved tougher. Gonzaga didn't reach the Elite Eight until 2015.

Two years later, the Bulldogs broke through and reached the national championship game with a 37–1 record. Facing blue blood North Carolina, Gonzaga led 65–63 with under two minutes to go. However, the Bulldogs didn't score again and lost 71–65.

As Gonzaga's profile improved, Few was able to attract top high school recruits. Few also broke a college basketball trend by staying at Gonzaga. Though many bigger schools wanted to hire him, Few turned them down. Instead, he

THE STREAK

In 2025, Gonzaga reached its 26th consecutive NCAA Tournament. The only school with a longer streak was Michigan State, with 27.

Bulldogs guard Jalen Suggs goes up for his deep game-winning shot in the 2021 Final Four.

stayed in Spokane and turned the Bulldogs into one of the nation's most successful programs.

In 2021, Few took a team with seven future NBA players on the roster to the Final Four. The Bulldogs were 30–0 entering their semifinal matchup against UCLA. Tied 90–90 with seconds left in overtime, Gonzaga guard Jalen Suggs raced to half-court. There, he was cut off by a defender. Suggs rose up and banked in a game-winning basket from well beyond the three-point line. The miracle shot propelled Gonzaga to the title game. But the Bulldogs were upended 86–70 by Baylor.

FACT BOX

First Season: 1907–08

Location: Spokane, Washington

Arena: McCarthey Athletic Center

Conference: West Coast Conference

All-Time Record: 1,842–1,128

NCAA Tournament Appearances: 26

Final Fours: 2

National Titles: None

Top Coaches: Dan Fitzgerald (1978–81, 1985–97); Dan Monson (1997–99); Mark Few (1999–)

Top Players: Frank Burgess (1958–61); John Stockton (1980–84); Jim McPhee (1985–90), Matt Santangelo (1996–2000); Ronny Turiaf (2001–05); Adam Morrison (2003–06); Kevin Pangos (2011–15); Drew Timme (2019–23)

Mascot: Spike the Bulldog

HOUSTON COUGARS

Center Elvin Hayes is mobbed by fans after Houston's upset win over UCLA in January 1968.

Houston played a key role in making college basketball a mainstream sport in the late 1960s. On January 20, 1968, the Cougars hosted UCLA. The Bruins had the sport's biggest star in center Lew Alcindor. UCLA had also won three of the previous four NCAA championships. The game was held at Houston's football/baseball stadium, the Astrodome, in front of more than 50,000 fans. Led by its own high-scoring star, center Elvin Hayes, Houston upset UCLA 71–69. The contest was dubbed "The Game of the Century."

That year, coach Guy Lewis took the Cougars to their second straight Final Four. But UCLA got revenge in the national semifinals. Lewis and Houston still didn't have a title by the early 1980s.

Akeem Olajuwon led the nation in blocks and rebounds in 1983–84.

BACK TO THE BIG TIME

Houston was an independent team for most of coach Guy Lewis's first two decades. The Cougars joined the powerful Southwest Conference in 1975. But when the conference broke up in 1996, Houston was left out of power conference basketball. The Cougars joined the smaller Conference USA and later the American Athletic Conference. Houston rejoined the power teams in 2023 when it was invited to the Big 12 Conference.

But the coach assembled one of the most talented and exciting teams in college basketball history. The Cougars featured 7-foot center Akeem Olajuwon (later Hakeem Olajuwon). Around him, Lewis had several athletic players. The team played an up-tempo style and threw down slam dunks often. One sportswriter made up a fake fraternity for the high-flying Cougars. He called it "Phi Slamma Jamma."

Houston's relentless defense helped the Cougars come from behind to beat Duke in the 2025 Final Four.

The Cougars reached the title game as heavy favorites against North Carolina State in 1983. But the Wolfpack slowed down the game. With Houston's speed game out of the picture, North Carolina State hung in. Houston lost 54–52 on a buzzer-beating dunk by North Carolina State's Lorenzo Charles. It was one of the biggest upsets in NCAA Tournament history.

The Cougars went back to the title game a year later. But Olajuwon was outdueled by Georgetown's star big man, Patrick Ewing. Houston lost 84–75.

FACT BOX

First Season: 1945–46

Location: Houston, Texas

Arena: Fertitta Center

Conference: Big 12 Conference

All-Time Record: 1,468–886

NCAA Tournament Appearances: 26

Final Fours: 7

National Titles: None

Top Coaches: Guy Lewis (1956–86); Pat Foster (1986–93); Kelvin Sampson (2014–)

Top Players: Elvin Hayes (1965–68); Don Chaney (1965–68); Otis Birdsong (1973–77); Clyde Drexler (1980–83); Michael Young (1980–84); Akeem Olajuwon (1981–84); Robert Gray (2015–18); Jamal Shead (2020–24)

Mascot: Shasta and Sasha

The Cougars didn't make it back to the Final Four until 2021 under Kelvin Sampson. Four years later, the veteran coach led Houston to another one. With their high-pressure defense, the Cougars rallied from 14 points down to shock Duke 70–67 in the national semifinals. However, Houston gave up a 12-point second-half lead against Florida in the championship game and ultimately lost 65–63.

Illinois had a strong basketball program in the first half of the 1900s. Starting in 1907–08, the team began a run of 52 seasons with only two losing records. And once the NCAA Tournament began in 1939, the Illini were frequent competitors. They reached the Final Four in both 1949 and 1951 under coach Harry Combes.

Combes coached Illinois for 20 seasons. The school's next long-term coach signed up in 1975. Lou Henson spent 21 years on the bench and had only two losing seasons. His 1988–89 Illini team thrilled fans

Coach Lou Henson had a 423–224 record over his career at Illinois from 1975 to 1996.

all year. Guard Nick Anderson and forward Kenny Battle led a fast-paced offense that averaged 86.4 points per game. Legendary commentator Dick Vitale dubbed the squad "The Flyin' Illini."

The team earned a No. 1 seed in the NCAA Tournament after finishing 26–4. Anderson and Battle then combined for 52 points in an 89–86 win over Syracuse to reach the Final Four. However, in the national semifinals, the Illini were beaten 83–81 by eventual champion Michigan.

The next great NCAA Tournament

Illinois guard Nick Anderson goes up for a basket against Missouri in 1989.

Illinois guard Luther Head lays the ball up during the team's comeback win over Arizona in the 2005 Elite Eight.

run for Illinois came in 2005. Second-year coach Bruce Weber guided the Illini to a 33–1 record in the regular season. The team featured a high-scoring three-guard lineup of Dee Brown, Luther Head, and Deron Williams.

Illinois trailed Arizona by 15 with 4:04 left in the Elite Eight. The Illini then smothered the Wildcats. Illinois rallied to force overtime and then won 90–89. Illinois eventually reached the championship game but fell to North Carolina 75–70. The team didn't reach another regional final until 2024.

THE WHIZ KIDS

One of the best teams in Illinois history never got the chance to compete in postseason play. The 1942–43 squad became known as "The Whiz Kids" as it raced to a 17–1 record. However, by then the United States was fighting in World War II (1939–45). And at the end of the regular season, three of Illinois's star players, Art Mathisen, Ken Menke, and Jack Smiley, were drafted into the military. Without its full lineup, Illinois turned down both the NCAA and NIT tournaments.

FACT BOX

First Season: 1905–06

Location: Champaign, Illinois

Arena: State Farm Center

Conference: Big Ten Conference

All-Time Record: 1,906–1,061

NCAA Tournament Appearances: 35

Final Fours: 5

National Titles: None

Top Coaches: Harry Combes (1947–67); Lou Henson (1975–96); Bruce Weber (2003–12)

Top Players: Andy Phillip (1941–43, 1946–47); Nick Anderson (1987–89); Deon Thomas (1990–94); Kiwane Garris (1993–97); Dee Brown (2002–06); Deron Williams (2002–05); Malcolm Hill (2013–17); Ayo Dosunmu (2018–21)

Mascot: None

INDIANA HOOSIERS

Indiana coach Branch McCracken talks to his players, including three-time All-American Don Schlundt, *second from right*, in 1953.

The basketball-mad state of Indiana is home to 11 Division I men's programs. But none can match the success of the state's biggest university. The NCAA Tournament was first played in 1939. A year later, the Hoosiers claimed their first title. Coach Branch McCracken was still on the bench when the team won again in 1953.

Though McCracken enjoyed success over more than two decades at Indiana, Hoosiers basketball is most associated with Bobby Knight. The demanding coach was hired in 1971. A former coach at Army, Knight ran his teams with military precision. He demanded perfection, and in 1975–76 his team delivered. Led by All-America forward Scott May and center Kent Benson, the Hoosiers finished the season 27–0. They then won five NCAA Tournament games to claim the championship. Three of the tournament wins were by double-digit margins, including an 86–68 victory over rival Michigan in the final. In nearly 50 seasons since, no men's team has matched Indiana's perfect season.

Behind superstar point guard Isiah Thomas, Knight's Hoosiers won another title in 1981. The team went back to the final in 1987. This time, guard Keith Smart's basket with four seconds remaining delivered a 74–73 win over Syracuse.

Forward Scott May, *center*, celebrates Indiana's 1976 national championship with coach Bobby Knight, *left*, and guard Quinn Buckner.

Knight coached the Hoosiers until 2000. He missed the NCAA Tournament only four times. But over the years, his legendary temper became an issue. In one 1985 game, Knight famously tossed a chair across the court to protest a call. And he often screamed at reporters. In 2000, a tape surfaced that showed Knight grabbing guard Neil Reed near Reed's throat

Calbert Cheaney became Indiana's all-time leading scorer in 1993. The guard finished his career with 2,613 points.

during a practice. That September, the school fired him for his "continued pattern of unacceptable behavior."

With fans still reeling from Knight's firing, the team made a surprise run to the national title game in 2002 under new coach Mike Davis. But the Hoosiers fell 64–52 to Maryland. For the next two decades, Indiana went through six head coaches, but none could get the team back to the top.

FACT BOX

First Season: 1900–01

Location: Bloomington, Indiana

Arena: Simon Skjodt Assembly Hall

Conference: Big Ten Conference

All-Time Record: 1,950–1,130

NCAA Tournament Appearances: 41

Final Fours: 8

National Titles: 1940, 1953, 1976, 1981, 1987

Top Coaches: Branch McCracken (1938–43, 1946–65); Bobby Knight (1971–2000); Mike Davis (2000–06)

Top Players: Don Schlundt (1951–55); Scott May (1973–76); Kent Benson (1973–77); Isiah Thomas (1979–81); Steve Alford (1983–87); Calbert Cheaney (1989–93); A. J. Guyton (1996–2000); Trayce Jackson-Davis (2019–23)

Mascot: None

UNIFORM TRADITIONS

Indiana's uniforms have never featured players' names on their backs. When coach Mike Davis suggested they be added in 2002, fans stood by the traditional look. They said they didn't want the change, and the idea was quickly abandoned. Indiana's most recognizable uniform item is the team's warm-up pants. The team began wearing the red-and-white-striped pants in the 1970s.

KANSAS JAYHAWKS

The basketball program at Kansas was founded in 1898 by the same man who invented the sport, Dr. James Naismith. Naismith finished his nine seasons in charge of the Jayhawks with a losing record of 55–60. None of the other ten coaches in program history finished under .500. Kansas has the most wins of any Division I program.

Forrest "Phog" Allen took over for Naismith. He left after two years but returned in 1919 and stayed in the position until 1956. He led the Jayhawks to their first national championship in 1952. Allen is known as "The Father of Basketball Coaching."

Despite having many strong seasons, Kansas didn't win another title until 1988. Coach Larry Brown's Jayhawks entered the tournament as a No. 6 seed. But led by All-America senior forward Danny Manning, Kansas upset in-state rival Kansas State as well as Duke on its way to the championship game. Manning then put up 31 points and 18 rebounds in an 83–79 title-clinching win over Oklahoma.

Kansas's home arena is named Allen Fieldhouse in honor of former coach Phog Allen, *right*.

Danny Manning led a Jayhawks team nicknamed "Danny and the Miracles" to the 1988 NCAA title.

Kansas needed another 30 years to get back on top. With time running out in the 2008 championship game, the Jayhawks trailed Memphis 63–60. Kansas guard Mario Chalmers hit a tough three-pointer over Tigers star Derrick Rose with 2.1 seconds left to tie the game. The Jayhawks then took control in overtime to win 75–68.

That victory came under coach Bill Self. The veteran coach took Kansas back to the Final Four in 2012 and 2018. However, the 2018 appearance was later voided by the NCAA due to a recruiting scandal. Self and Kansas finally broke through again in 2022. The Jayhawks faced former coach Roy Williams and North Carolina in the championship game. Kansas erased a 15-point halftime deficit to win 72–69 and capture the storied program's fourth title.

Kansas guard Mario Chalmers lines up his game-tying shot in the 2008 NCAA title game against Memphis.

ROCK CHALK JAYHAWK

Kansas basketball fans open each game by chanting "Rock Chalk Jayhawk." The cheer originated in 1886 as "Rah Rah Jayhawk." But the first two words were eventually changed to create the rhyme. When Kansas is comfortably ahead late in games, fans will begin a slow chant before eventually speeding up to celebrate the certain victory.

FACT BOX

First Season: 1898–99

Location: Lawrence, Kansas

Arena: Allen Fieldhouse

Conference: Big 12 Conference

All-Time Record: 2,414–909

NCAA Tournament Appearances: 52

Final Fours: 15

National Titles: 1952, 1988, 2008, 2022

Top Coaches: Phog Allen (1907–09, 1919–56); Roy Williams (1988–2003); Bill Self (2003–)

Top Players: Clyde Lovellette (1949–52); Wilt Chamberlain (1956–58); Danny Manning (1984–88); Raef LaFrentz (1994–98); Nick Collison (1999–2003); Sherron Collins (2006–10); Ochai Agbaji (2018–22)

Mascot: Big Jay, Baby Jay

KENTUCKY WILDCATS

Few schools can boast as impressive a basketball history as Kentucky. Through 2025, the Wildcats were second in total wins among Division I men's teams. Kentucky had appeared in more NCAA Tournaments than any other program. And the Wildcats' eight national titles ranked second only to UCLA.

Kentucky's greatest era lasted more than four decades. Under coach Adolph Rupp from 1930 to 1970, the Wildcats never had a losing season.

Kentucky fans celebrate the program's 2,000th win in 2009.

Rupp's "Fabulous Five" of Cliff Barker, Ralph Beard, Alex Groza, Wallace Jones, and Kenny Rollins won the 1948 NCAA title. With Rollins gone, the other four led the Wildcats to another championship in 1949. Kentucky won again in 1951 and 1958. Rupp coached another 14 years and left as college basketball's all-time wins leader with 876. Today, the Wildcats play their games in Rupp Arena.

Adolph Rupp was known as "The Baron of the Bluegrass" during his time coaching Kentucky from 1930 to 1972.

One stain on Rupp's legacy was his refusal to recruit Black players. During his time, Kentucky had only one Black player, and he stayed only one season. Rupp's replacement, Joe B. Hall, was eager to show the Wildcats could be a program for everybody. One way he did this was by hiring the team's first Black assistant coach. Before long, Black players were essential in keeping the Wildcats a top program. Hall led Kentucky to another title in 1978. Hall's teams played an

THE UNFORGETTABLES

While on probation, Kentucky was banned from the 1990 and 1991 NCAA Tournaments. But Richie Farmer, Deron Feldhaus, John Pelphrey, and Sean Woods all stuck with the program. As seniors in 1991–92, they led the Wildcats to the Elite Eight before losing to Duke on a stunning last-second shot. The four players are known to Kentucky fans as "The Unforgettables" for their commitment to rebuilding the team.

up-tempo style. They were frequently near the top of national scoring lists.

By the late 1980s, the Wildcats began to struggle. The program was on probation in 1989 when Rick Pitino took over. In 1996, Pitino led Kentucky back to the top. His deep, talented team was called "The Untouchables." With ten future NBA players, the Wildcats beat Syracuse 76–67 for the championship. Pitino left for the NBA a year later, but the Wildcats won another NCAA title in 1998 under Tubby Smith.

After struggling in the early 2000s, Kentucky brought in coach John Calipari in 2009. At the time, many young basketball stars were spending only one year in college before leaving for the NBA. Calipari leaned into these top recruits. He often started five freshmen. In 2011–12, Calipari's young team was led by center Anthony Davis. The 6-foot, 10-inch Davis had 18 points, 14 rebounds, and five blocks in a Final Four win over rival Louisville. He then grabbed 16 rebounds, blocked six shots, and dished out five assists in a 67–59 championship-game win over Kansas.

FACT BOX

First Season: 1902–03

Location: Lexington, Kentucky

Arena: Rupp Arena

Conference: Southeastern Conference

All-Time Record: 2,422–770–1

NCAA Tournament Appearances: 62

Final Fours: 17

National Titles: 1948, 1949, 1951, 1958, 1978, 1996, 1998, 2012

Top Coaches: Adolph Rupp (1930–72); Joe B. Hall (1972–85); Rick Pitino (1989–97); John Calipari (2009–24)

Top Players: Alex Groza (1945, 1946–49); Ralph Beard (1945–49); Frank Ramsey (1950–52, 1954); Dan Issel (1967–70); Jack Givens (1975–78); Kenny Walker (1982–86); Jamal Mashburn (1990–93); Anthony Davis (2011–12)

Mascot: The Wildcat

Kentucky forward Anthony Davis goes up for a shot in the 2012 NCAA title game against Kansas.

LOUISVILLE CARDINALS

Louisville native Charlie Tyra scored 1,728 points and grabbed a school-record 1,617 rebounds for the Cardinals between 1953 and 1957.

The Louisville Cardinals and neighboring Kentucky Wildcats have a fierce rivalry. And while Kentucky has a deeper history, Louisville has a storied basketball tradition of its own. The Cardinals first became a contender in 1945–46 when coach Peck Hickman led the team to 22 wins. Hickman stayed on the bench until 1967. He never had a losing season in charge of Louisville.

Denny Crum took over in 1971 and eventually passed Hickman's school record of 443 wins. Crum led the Cardinals to the Final Four in his first season. It was the first of six Final Four appearances in 15 years for Crum, who coached Louisville through the 2000–01 season.

Crum's teams fell in the semifinals of both the 1972 and 1975 Final Fours.

But Crum's Cardinals broke through in 1980. Louisville beat Iowa in the semifinals. Led by high-flying guard Darrell Griffith's 23 points, the Cardinals then upended UCLA 59–54 for the school's first championship.

After Final Four berths in 1982 and 1983, Louisville made it back to the championship game in 1986. This time the Cardinals rallied to beat underdog LSU in the semifinals. Louisville then came from behind at halftime to beat Duke 72–69 in the title game.

Guard Darrell Griffith is carried off the court after Louisville's win in the 1980 NCAA title game.

NEVER NERVOUS

Freshman Pervis Ellison was one of the stars of Louisville's 1986 championship run. The 6-foot, 9-inch center had double-doubles in each of the Cardinals' last three tournament games. He put up 25 points and grabbed 11 rebounds in the final against Duke. Along the way, Ellison was nicknamed "Never Nervous Pervis" for his calm play. He became the first freshman in 42 years to win the Final Four Most Outstanding Player Award.

Coach Denny Crum, *right*, had only three losing seasons in 30 years at Louisville from 1971 to 2001.

Another legendary coach, Rick Pitino, took over for Crum in 2001. It was a surprising hire. Pitino had recently coached for eight seasons at archrival Kentucky, where he led the Wildcats to the 1996 NCAA title. At Louisville, Pitino led the Cardinals to three Final Four appearances. In 2013, they knocked off Michigan 82–76 to win their third NCAA championship. However, the title was later stripped by the NCAA after a recruiting scandal. Louisville became the first team to have a title taken away.

Pitino was fired in 2017 after a second scandal. Louisville was placed on probation. Through the struggles, the team's record suffered. In 2024–25, new coach Pat Kelsey took the team back to the NCAA Tournament for the first time in six years. That broke Louisville's longest tournament drought since the 1950s.

FACT BOX

First Season: 1911–12

Location: Louisville, Kentucky

Arena: KFC Yum! Center

Conference: Atlantic Coast Conference

All-Time Record: 1,811–1,019

NCAA Tournament Appearances: 40

Final Fours: 8

National Titles: 1980, 1986

Top Coaches: Peck Hickman (1944–67); Denny Crum (1971–2001); Rick Pitino (2001–17)

Top Players: Charlie Tyra (1953–57); Wes Unseld (1965–68); Junior Bridgeman (1972–75); Darrell Griffith (1976–80); Milt Wagner (1981–86); Pervis Ellison (1985–89); DeJuan Wheat (1993–97); Russ Smith (2010–14)

Mascot: Louie the Cardinal

LOYOLA (IL) RAMBLERS

For much of its history, Loyola has been an underdog basketball program. But the Chicago-based Ramblers have provided a handful of lasting NCAA Tournament memories. The first came in 1963. At the time, college basketball was still highly segregated. Many coaches did not recruit Black players. Others went by a so-called "gentlemen's agreement" to put no more than three Black players on the court at one time.

Coach George Ireland's 1963 Loyola team helped break down racial barriers in college basketball.

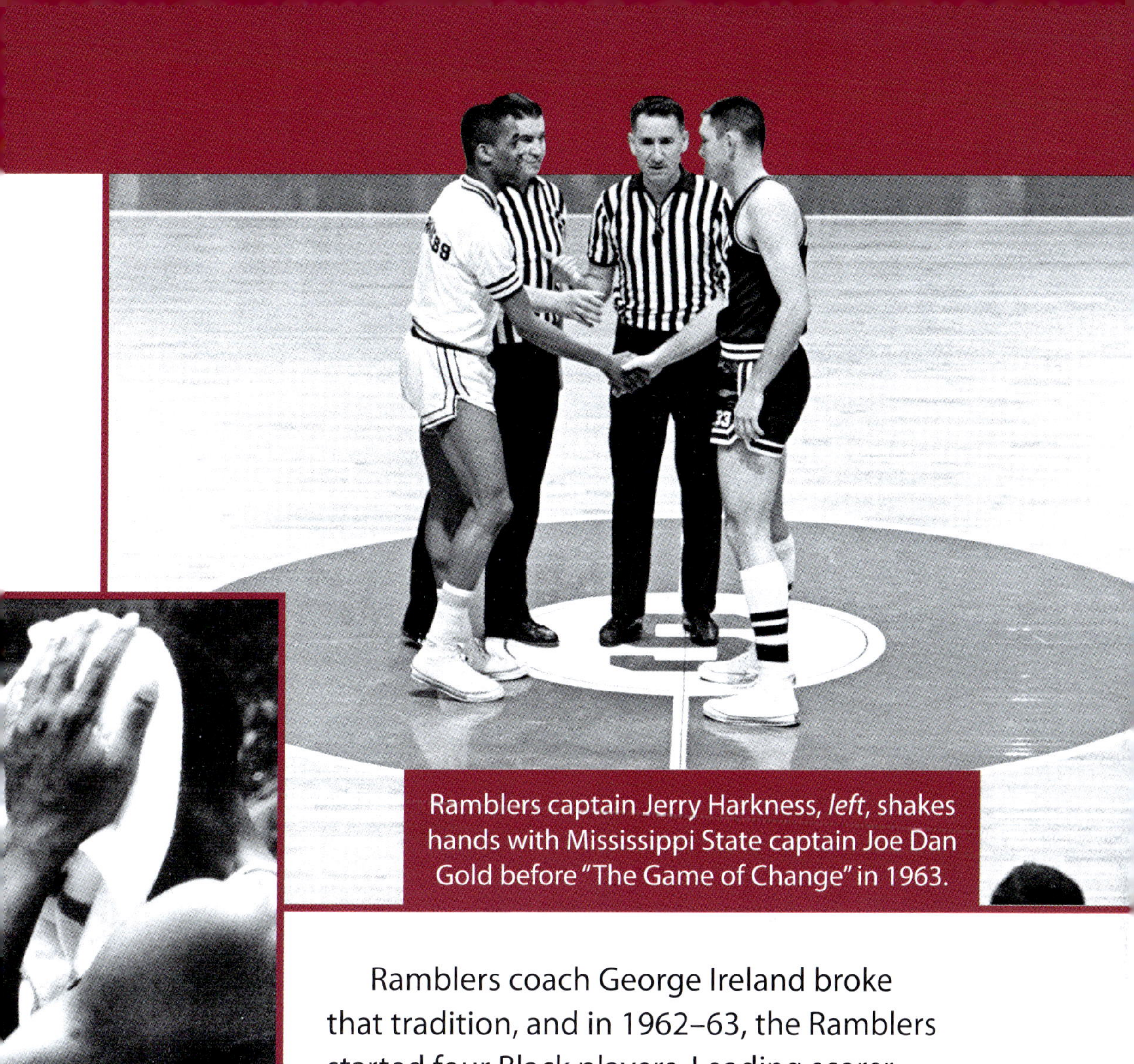

Ramblers captain Jerry Harkness, *left*, shakes hands with Mississippi State captain Joe Dan Gold before "The Game of Change" in 1963.

Ramblers coach George Ireland broke that tradition, and in 1962–63, the Ramblers started four Black players. Leading scorer Jerry Harkness, Les Hunter, Ron Miller, and Vic Rouse all averaged at least 13 points per game. Loyola finished 29–2. In the second round of the NCAA Tournament, the Ramblers were set to face all-white Mississippi State. The Bulldogs were ordered by the governor of Mississippi to stay home. But the team played the game anyway. Loyola won 61–51 in what was later

Loyola's Donte Ingram celebrates his game-winning three-pointer against Miami in the 2018 NCAA Tournament.

SISTER JEAN

Loyola's team chaplain became a national celebrity during the Ramblers' Final Four run in 2018. Sister Jean Dolores Schmidt was 98 years old during the tournament. She sat near the team's bench during every tournament game and even talked strategy. Sister Jean and Loyola returned to the tournament in 2021. However, she could not sit with the team due to the COVID-19 pandemic.

dubbed "The Game of Change." After routing Duke 94–75 in the semifinals, the Ramblers capped off their groundbreaking tournament by beating two-time defending champion Cincinnati 60–58. Hunter and Rouse each posted double-doubles. Rouse won the game with a tip-in at the buzzer.

The Ramblers' next great tournament run came in 2018. Coach Porter Moser's team entered the tournament as an unknown No. 11 seed. But on its run to the Final Four, Loyola became a fan favorite. The team hit late game-winning shots in three straight games. In the opening round, forward Donte Ingram hit a long three-pointer just before the buzzer to beat Miami 64–62. Then guard Clayton Custer hit a floating 15-foot jump shot with four seconds left to upset Tennessee 63–62 in the second round. With six seconds left in the Sweet 16 against Nevada, guard Marques Townes hit a three-pointer for a 69–68 Ramblers win. Loyola then routed Kansas State 78–62 to reach the Final Four. There, the team's run ended with a 69–57 loss to Michigan.

FACT BOX

First Season: 1913–14

Location: Chicago, Illinois

Arena: Gentile Arena

Conference: Atlantic 10 Conference

All-Time Record: 1,472–1,242

NCAA Tournament Appearances: 8

Final Fours: 2

National Titles: 1963

Top Coaches: Leonard Sachs (1923–42); George Ireland (1951–75); Porter Moser (2011–21)

Top Players: Nick Kladis (1949–52); Jerry Harkness (1960–63), John Egan (1961–64); Vic Rouse (1961–64); Ron Miller (1961–64); Les Hunter (1961–64); Alfredrick Hughes (1981–85); Cameron Krutwig (2017–21)

Mascot: LU Wolf

LSU TIGERS

LSU guard "Pistol" Pete Maravich averaged an NCAA-record 44.2 points per game from 1967 to 1970.

Basketball fans in Baton Rouge have witnessed some of the most dominant players ever to take a college basketball court. From 1967 to 1970, "Pistol" Pete Maravich thrilled Louisiana State University (LSU) fans with his effortless scoring. Maravich played at a time when freshmen could not play for varsity teams. He also played before the shot clock and the three-point shot were part of college basketball. Despite those limits, Maravich used his exceptional quickness and ballhandling to create his own shots from anywhere on the floor. In three seasons, he set the NCAA record with 3,667 points.

Two decades later, towering center Shaquille O'Neal overpowered opponents. O'Neal stood 7-feet, 1-inch tall and weighed nearly 300 pounds. But he could handle the ball well and sprint up the floor with the speed of most guards. As a sophomore in 1990–91, O'Neal averaged an SEC-leading

LSU center Shaquille O'Neal overpowered defenders with his thunderous dunks.

27.6 points per game. He led the nation with 14.7 rebounds per game. He also blocked five shots per game. The next season, he was named an All-American for the second time after averaging more than 24 points, 14 rebounds, and five blocks again.

Neither Maravich nor O'Neal ever played in a Final Four. But LSU has made four runs to that round. The first came in 1953 under longtime coach Harry Rabenhorst. The program's winningest team was coached by Dale Brown in the 1981 tournament. The 31–5 Tigers were a No. 1 seed and blew out three opponents before losing to eventual champion Indiana in the national semifinals. In 1986, Brown's Tigers were seeded No. 11. They became the first double-digit seed ever to reach the Final Four.

BIG UPSETS

In 1986, LSU had to beat all three of the top seeds in the Southeast region to reach the Final Four. The Tigers beat No. 3 seed Memphis State 83–81 in the second round. LSU then beat No. 2 seed Georgia Tech in the Sweet 16. The final upset was a 59–57 win over top-seeded Kentucky in the Elite Eight. Nearly 40 years later, no other No. 11 seed had ever beaten all three top seeds in one region of the NCAA Tournament.

Forward Glen Davis salutes LSU's fans after the Tigers beat Texas to reach the 2006 Final Four.

Coach John Brady led LSU back to the Final Four in 2006. His team was led by Glen "Big Baby" Davis. The 6-foot, 9-inch, 290-pound forward had three 20-point games in LSU's four tournament wins. The No. 4–seeded Tigers knocked off Texas 70–60 in overtime in the Elite Eight. However, a 59–45 loss to UCLA in the next round ended LSU's run.

FACT BOX

First Season: 1908–09

Location: Baton Rouge, Louisiana

Arena: Pete Maravich Assembly Center

Conference: Southeastern Conference

All-Time Record: 1,665–1,270

NCAA Tournament Appearances: 24

Final Fours: 4

National Titles: None

Top Coaches: Harry Rabenhorst (1925–42, 1945–57); Dale Brown (1972–97); John Brady (1997–2008)

Top Players: Bob Pettit (1951–54); Pete Maravich (1967–70); Rudy Macklin (1976–81); Howard Carter (1979–83); Mahmoud Abdul-Rauf (1988–90); Shaquille O'Neal (1989–92); Glen Davis (2004–07); Tasmin Mitchell (2005–10)

Mascot: Mike the Tiger

MARQUETTE GOLDEN EAGLES

Marquette's first taste of success came in the 1970 NIT. That year, the team's charismatic coach, Al McGuire, turned down the NCAA Tournament because he didn't like Marquette's bracket draw. Instead, the team beat Saint John's 65–53 to win the NIT title.

Coach Al McGuire had a record of 295–80 in 13 seasons at Marquette from 1964 to 1977.

That was the first of McGuire's NCAA Tournament adventures. In the 1974 championship game against North Carolina State, he was given two technical fouls. McGuire blamed his outbursts after Marquette lost 76–64.

Three years later, McGuire led a talented team back to the Final Four. In the semifinals, Marquette and Charlotte were tied 49–49 with three seconds left. Inbounding under his own basket, Marquette guard

Butch Lee heaved a floor-length pass to center Jerome Whitehead, who laid the ball in just before time expired for a dramatic 51–49 win. Lee then led the way in the championship game. The Final Four Most Outstanding Player scored 19 points in a 67–59 win over North Carolina.

The popular McGuire retired after the win. For more than two decades, the team struggled to get back to the top. In 2003, talented guard Dwyane Wade led a No. 3–seeded team into the NCAA Tournament. Wade put on a memorable performance in the Elite Eight against Kentucky. He had 29 points on 11-of-16

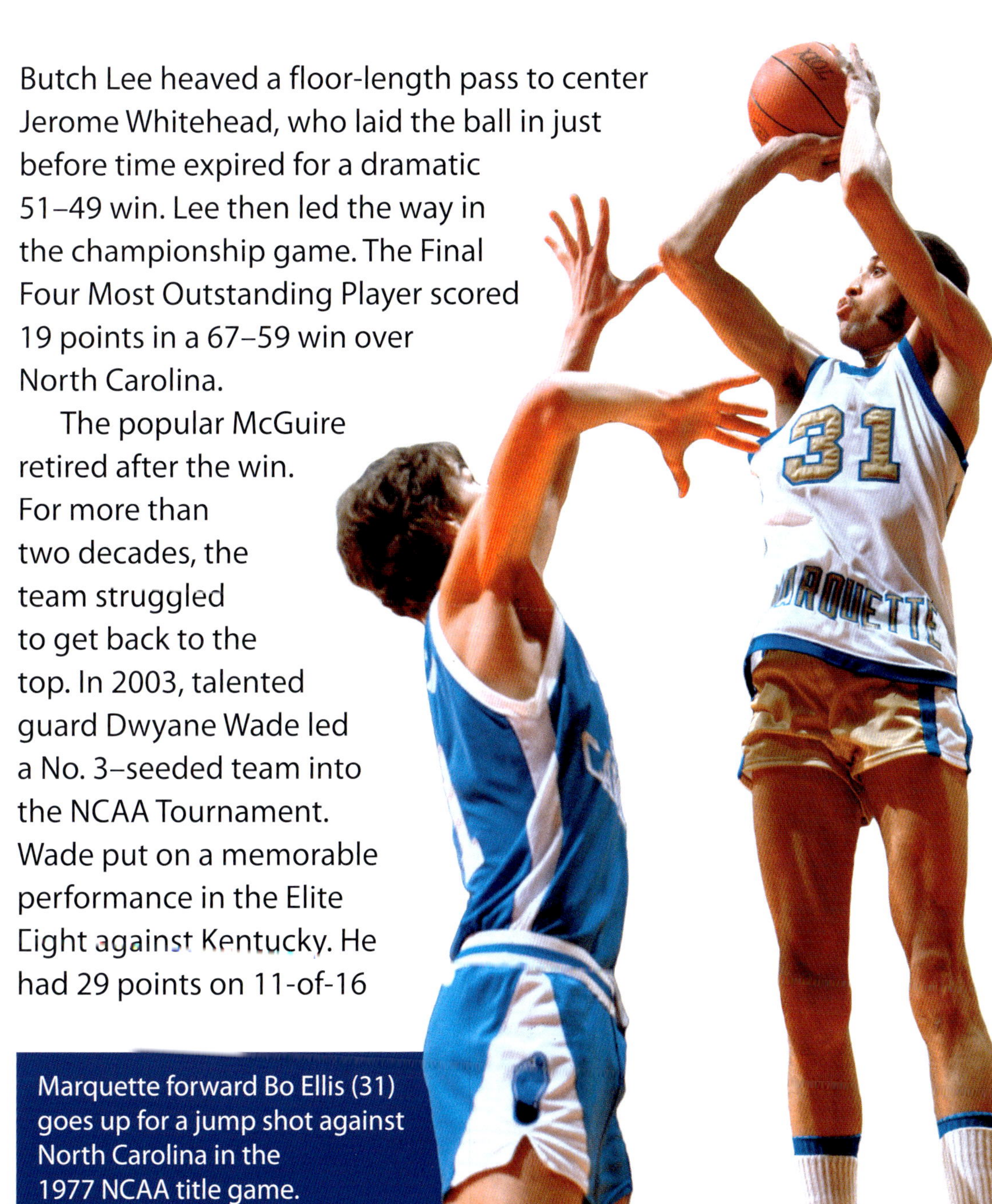

Marquette forward Bo Ellis (31) goes up for a jump shot against North Carolina in the 1977 NCAA title game.

Golden Eagles guard Dwyane Wade surges past a Kentucky defender during the 2003 Elite Eight.

shooting and added 11 rebounds and 11 assists. It was just the fifth recorded triple-double in NCAA Tournament history. However, the Golden Eagles were upended 94–61 in the national semifinals by Kansas.

The Final Four run helped the Golden Eagles jump from the smaller Conference USA to the powerful Big East in 2005. Marquette captured its first regular-season Big East title in 2013. That same year, the Golden Eagles reached the Elite Eight, their deepest run since the 2003 Final Four. Their next deep run came in 2024, when coach Shaka Smart led the team back to the Sweet 16.

CHANGING NAMES

From 1954 to 1994, Marquette's nickname was the Warriors. But after protests from American Indian groups, the school changed to the Golden Eagles. In 2005, the school briefly adopted the nickname "Gold." But the nickname was so unpopular with students that Marquette went back to Golden Eagles before ever using the new name in a game.

FACT BOX

First Season: 1916–17

Location: Milwaukee, Wisconsin

Arena: Fiserv Forum

Conference: Big East Conference

All-Time Record: 1,763–1,073

NCAA Tournament Appearances: 37

Final Fours: 3

National Titles: 1977

Top Coaches: Al McGuire (1964–77); Hank Raymonds (1977–83); Tom Crean (1999–2008)

Top Players: Don Kojis (1958–61); Maurice Lucas (1972–74); Bo Ellis (1973–77); Butch Lee (1974–78); Dwyane Wade (2001–03); Jerel McNeal (2005–09); Dominic James (2005–09); Markus Howard (2016–20)

Mascot: Iggy

MARYLAND TERRAPINS

Maryland was a founding member of the ACC in 1953. But the Terrapins struggled to contend in the tough conference for the first two decades. That finally changed after coach Charles "Lefty" Driesell took over a losing program in the late 1960s. By 1973, the popular Driesell and a team led by center Len Elmore, guard John Lucas, and forward Tom McMillen reached the Elite Eight of the NCAA Tournament.

Driesell coached Maryland until 1986. He turned the Terps into respectable contenders. However, the team struggled again after he left. Gary Williams, a former Maryland point guard, took over in 1989. Williams had to deal with a harsh period of probation in the early 1990s. But by the middle of the decade, the Terrapins were regulars in the NCAA Tournament again.

Innovative Maryland coach Lefty Driesell gathered his players at midnight on the first day practices were allowed in 1971–72. Soon, many schools copied the "Midnight Madness" tradition.

In 2001, Maryland reached the Final Four as a No. 3 seed. At one point in the first half, the Terrapins led conference rival Duke by 22 points. However, the No. 1 seed Blue Devils came back to win.

Maryland was back with a strong lineup in 2001–02. Slick-passing point guard Steve Blake fed high-scoring guard Juan Dixon and physical forward Lonny Baxter. After finishing 26–4 and earning a No. 1 seed, Maryland had to face several strong programs in the NCAA Tournament. The Terrapins beat Kentucky in the Sweet 16 and Connecticut in the Elite Eight. Maryland then knocked off Kansas to set up a matchup with Indiana in the championship game.

Guard Juan Dixon left Maryland in 2002 as the school's all-time leading scorer with 2,269 points.

Dixon led the way with 18 points. Baxter added 15 points and 14 rebounds. Normally a high-scoring team, the Terrapins clamped down on defense to win 64–52 and claim the title.

Williams coached until 2011. Four seasons later, the Terrapins left the ACC to join the Big Ten. In 2025, Maryland

Coach Gary Williams, *center*, celebrates with his team after Maryland's national-championship victory over Indiana in 2002.

reached the Sweet 16. However, the team lost to top-seeded Florida, continuing a streak of not advancing past that round since its 2002 title.

AN EPIC SHOWDOWN

In 1974, Maryland was ranked No. 4 in the country when it took on North Carolina State in the ACC Tournament final. At the time, only conference tournament winners and independents reached the NCAA Tournament. North Carolina State won an epic game 103–100 in overtime. The game helped push the NCAA toward expanding its tournament field to include more top teams.

FACT BOX

First Season: 1910–11

Location: College Park, Maryland

Arena: Xfinity Center

Conference: Big Ten Conference

All-Time Record: 1,687–1,143 (96)

NCAA Tournament Appearances: 30

Final Fours: 2

National Titles: 2002

Top Coaches: Bud Millikan (1950–67); Lefty Driesell (1969–86); Gary Williams (1989–2011)

Top Players: Len Elmore (1971–74); Tom McMillen (1971–74); John Lucas (1972–76); Albert King (1977–81); Len Bias (1982–86); Joe Smith (1993–95); Juan Dixon (1998–2002); Greivis Vasquez (2006–10)

Mascot: Testudo

MEMPHIS TIGERS

After starring as a player for Memphis State in the 1970s, Larry Finch coached the Tigers from 1986 to 1997.

The Memphis Tigers boast one of the top winning percentages in men's college basketball. However, the team has never won the NCAA Tournament. The Tigers have come close on three occasions. The first came in 1973, when the school was known as Memphis State. Coach Gene Bartow's high-scoring team featured guard Larry Finch, forward Larry Kenon, and center Ronnie Robinson. The Tigers reached the championship game before falling to UCLA 87–66.

Memphis State earned a No. 2 seed in the 1985 tournament. The Tigers then survived three straight games decided by two points or less. The third, a 63–61 win over No. 1 seed Oklahoma, put the

Tigers back in the Final Four. There, Memphis State was upset 52–45 by eventual champion Villanova.

The school shortened its name to Memphis in 1994. The team was struggling when John Calipari took over in 2000. By 2008, Calipari had a 38–1 squad in the NCAA championship game again. Sensational freshman guard Derrick Rose led Memphis to a three-point lead over Kansas with seconds to play. However, the Tigers gave up a game-tying three-pointer at the buzzer and lost 75–68 in overtime.

However, two of Memphis's most successful seasons have also been shrouded in controversy. The coach of the 1985 team, Dana Kirk, was caught paying players, which was against the rules at the time. As a result, the NCAA removed the team's Final Four appearance from the

Memphis guard Derrick Rose goes up for a layup against UCLA in the 2008 Final Four.

Penny Hardaway was an All-America point guard for Memphis State during the 1992–93 season. He later returned as the team's coach.

record books. The team's 2008 runner-up finish was later voided as well. This time, the NCAA ruled that Rose had been ineligible during the 2007–08 season due to questions about his SAT scores. The Tigers had been the first men's team ever to win 38 games in a season. Instead, Memphis was forced to forfeit all of its games, and those records were wiped away.

Memphis struggled to get back to an elite level after Calipari left in 2009. In 2018, the Tigers hired former star point guard Penny Hardaway as coach. Hardaway led the team to 20 wins in six of his first seven seasons.

FACT BOX

First Season: 1920–21

Location: Memphis, Tennessee

Arena: FedExForum

Conference: American Athletic Conference

All-Time Record: 1,702–971–1

NCAA Tournament Appearances: 23

Final Fours: 1

National Titles: None

Top Coaches: Gene Bartow (1970–74); Larry Finch (1986–97); John Calipari (2000–09)

Top Players: Forest Arnold (1952–56); Larry Finch (1970–73); Keith Lee (1981–85); Elliot Perry (1987–91); Anfernee "Penny" Hardaway (1991–93); Rodney Carney (2002–06); Chris Douglas-Roberts (2005–08); Derrick Rose (2007–08)

Mascot: Pouncer

NIT WINNERS

The Tigers have claimed a pair of NIT championships in their history. In 2002, coach John Calipari led Memphis to a 72–62 win over South Carolina. In 2021, Penny Hardaway's Tigers knocked off Mississippi State 77–64.

MICHIGAN WOLVERINES

The Michigan Wolverines first reached the Final Four in 1964. A high-scoring team led by flashy forward Cazzie Russell lost in the national semifinals to Duke. Russell was named to the All-America team the following year as he carried Michigan to the 1965 final. There, the Wolverines fell 91–80 to UCLA. Michigan lost in the title game again in 1976, this time to conference rival Indiana.

Just before the 1989 NCAA Tournament began, Michigan coach Bill Frieder announced he was leaving after the season to coach Arizona State. Instead of waiting, Michigan athletic director Bo Schembechler fired Frieder and put assistant Steve Fisher in charge. Despite the sudden change, No. 3–seeded Michigan went on a run behind sharpshooter Glen Rice. The forward scored 31 points in the title game as Michigan outlasted Seton Hall 80–79 in overtime.

Michigan's Glen Rice fires a three-point shot against Seton Hall in the 1989 NCAA title game.

One of the most memorable periods in Michigan history began

in 1991–92, when Fisher brought in five talented freshmen. Guards Jalen Rose and Jimmy King, along with forwards Ray Jackson, Juwan Howard, and Chris Webber, shook up college basketball. At a time when few freshmen played big minutes, "The Fab Five" eventually became Michigan's starting lineup.

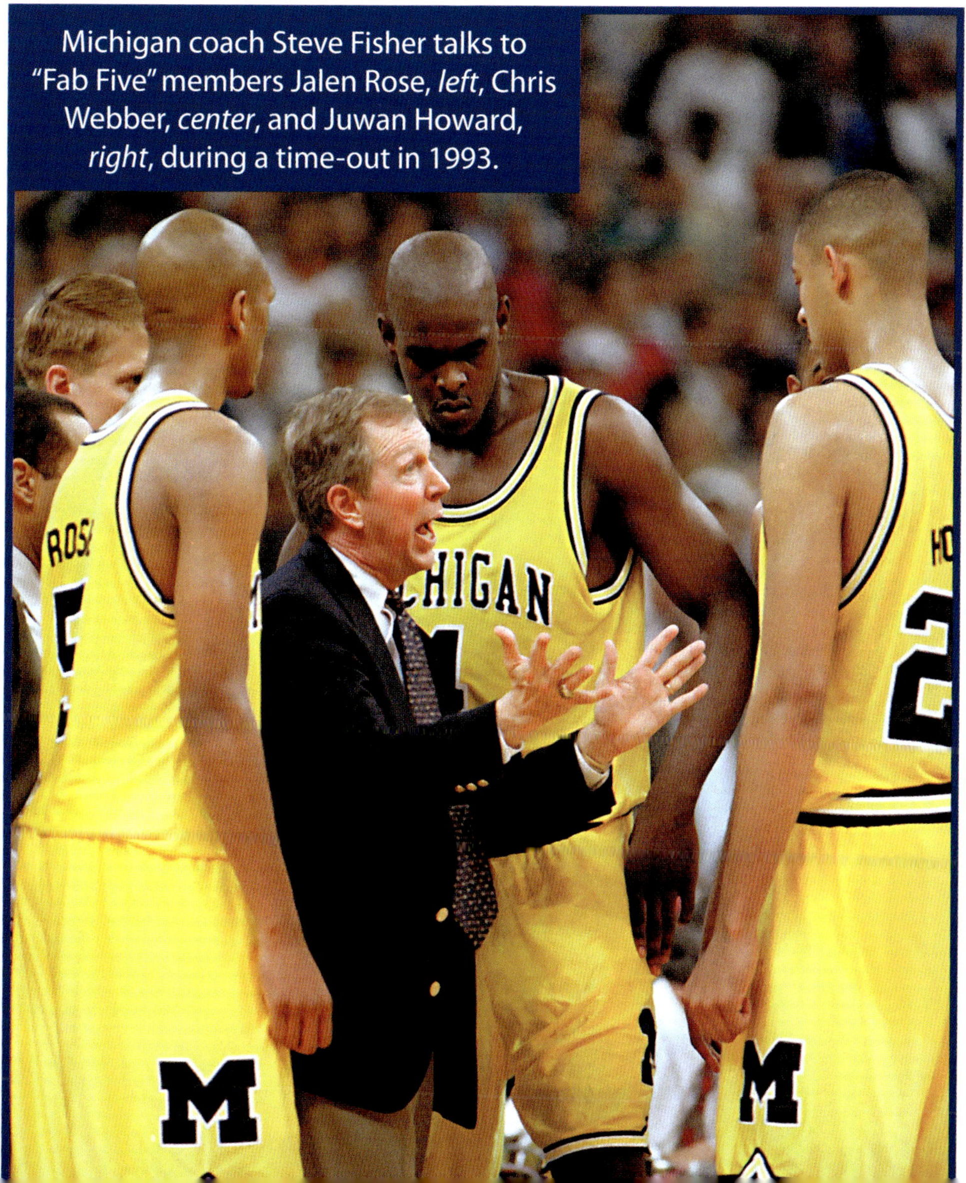

Michigan coach Steve Fisher talks to "Fab Five" members Jalen Rose, *left*, Chris Webber, *center*, and Juwan Howard, *right*, during a time-out in 1993.

With their baggy shorts and black shoes, the Fab Five upended college basketball fashion. They also won. Michigan got all the way to the NCAA championship game before falling 71–51 to Duke. With all five stars back, the Wolverines met North Carolina for the 1993 title. However, in the closing seconds, Webber called a time-out that Michigan didn't have. That was a technical foul. North Carolina went on to win 77–71.

Michigan didn't make it back to the championship game until 2013. The Wolverines were defeated 82–76 by Louisville. When the Cardinals were later stripped of the title for rules violations, many wondered whether it would be awarded to Michigan. The NCAA did not do so. And Michigan coach John Beilein said he wouldn't accept the trophy.

Guard Trey Burke became the first Michigan player to win the Naismith Award while leading the Wolverines to the NCAA title game in 2013.

SEVENTEEN POINTS OF FAME

Backup point guard Spike Albrecht averaged only 2.2 points in just over eight minutes per game in 2012–13. But Michigan called on the freshman in the national championship against Louisville after starter Trey Burke picked up early fouls. Albrecht shocked onlookers by scoring 17 points before halftime to keep Michigan in the game. Former Wolverines guard Jalen Rose was covering the game on television. At halftime, he jokingly compared Albrecht to legendary point guards Magic Johnson and Isiah Thomas.

FACT BOX

First Season: 1908–09

Location: Ann Arbor, Michigan

Arena: Crisler Center

Conference: Big Ten Conference

All-Time Record: 1,617–1,121

NCAA Tournament Appearances: 28

Final Fours: 6

National Titles: 1989

Top Coaches: Johnny Orr (1968–80); Steve Fisher (1989–97); John Beilein (2007–19)

Top Players: Bill Buntin (1962–65); Cazzie Russell (1963–66); Rudy Tomjanovich (1967–70); Phil Hubbard (1975–79); Mike McGee (1977–81); Glen Rice (1985–89); Jalen Rose (1991–94); Trey Burke (2011–13)

Mascot: None

MICHIGAN STATE SPARTANS

Michigan State needed nearly eight decades of basketball to become a national power. From the team's founding in 1898 until the 1970s, the Spartans' only Final Four appearance came in 1957. There they lost to eventual champion North Carolina.

Michigan State point guard Magic Johnson was an All-American in 1978–79 after averaging 17.1 points and 8.4 assists per game.

Michigan State coach Tom Izzo won his 700th career game in January 2024.

Things began to turn for the program when coach Jud Heathcote took over in 1976. After a 10–17 record in his first season, Heathcote recruited local star point guard Earvin "Magic" Johnson. In his sophomore season, Johnson led Michigan State to the top of the sport.

The Spartans were dominant in the 1979 NCAA Tournament, winning all five games by double-digit margins. That included a 75–64 victory over Indiana State in the championship game. The contest featured two of the sport's biggest stars ever in Johnson and Indiana State's Larry Bird. The game attracted a record TV audience and is often credited with making men's college basketball a popular sport nationally.

Heathcote stayed in East Lansing until 1995. But his teams never again got past the Sweet 16. Assistant Tom Izzo took over as head coach the next season. After reaching the Final Four in 1999, Izzo's team earned a top seed in 2000. Just as it had

21 years earlier, Michigan State dominated its opponents. Led by inspirational point guard Mateen Cleaves, the Spartans won all six games by at least 11 points. Cleaves was slowed by an ankle injury early in the second half of the title game against Florida. But he fought through the pain to lead Michigan State to an 89–76 win.

By the end of the 2018–19 season, Izzo had led Michigan State to the Final Four eight times. Though he had only one title, in 2000, he was recognized as one of the game's

Spartans point guard Mateen Cleaves was named the Most Outstanding Player of the 2000 NCAA Tournament.

THE FLINTSTONES

In the late 1990s, coach Tom Izzo had a strong recruiting pipeline to the blue-collar town of Flint, Michigan. At one point, four of Michigan State's players hailed from the city. Guards Mateen Cleaves and Charlie Bell and forward Morris Peterson were all key parts of the Spartans' 2000 championship team. The school's Flint players were known as "The Flintstones."

top coaches. He reached two milestones in 2025. First, Izzo passed Indiana's Bobby Knight as the all-time winningest coach in the Big Ten. Then, in March, the Spartans reached their 27th straight NCAA Tournament. That was the longest active streak in the nation. No. 2–seeded Michigan State rallied to beat Ole Miss 73–70 in the Sweet 16. It was Izzo's 59th NCAA Tournament win, the fourth most of any college coach.

FACT BOX

First Season: 1898–99

Location: East Lansing, Michigan

Arena: Breslin Center

Conference: Big Ten Conference

All-Time Record: 1,861–1,163

NCAA Tournament Appearances: 38

Final Fours: 10

National Titles: 1979, 2000

Top Coaches: Benjamin Van Alstyne (1926–49); Jud Heathcote (1976–95); Tom Izzo (1995–)

Top Players: Greg Kelser (1975–79); Magic Johnson (1977–79); Scott Skiles (1982–86); Steve Smith (1987–91); Shawn Respert (1991–95); Mateen Cleaves (1996–2000); Draymond Green (2008–12); Denzel Valentine (2012–16)

Mascot: Sparty

Michigan State's Magic Johnson, *left*, and Indiana State's Larry Bird helped raise the profile of college basketball.

Bird, *left*, and Johnson took their rivalry to the NBA next. Later in life, they became friends.

MAGIC VS. BIRD

The 1979 NCAA championship game featured two of college basketball's biggest stars. Crafty forward Larry Bird carried underdog Indiana State into the title game. Michigan State was led by Earvin "Magic" Johnson, a 6-foot-9-inch point guard who dazzled fans with his smooth ballhandling and slick passes.

The game ended up not being close. Behind a pressure defense, Michigan State controlled the game and won 75–64. Nonetheless, more than 35 million fans tuned in on television. It is still the highest-rated college basketball game ever. The game helped launch college basketball into a new era. By 1985, the tournament field had grown from 40 to 64. Many consider Magic vs. Bird the birth of "March Madness."

NORTH CAROLINA TAR HEELS

North Carolina's Dean E. Smith Center holds more than 21,000 fans.

Few schools can boast a stronger men's basketball tradition than North Carolina. Only Kansas and Kentucky have won more games. And no team has reached the Final Four more often than the Tar Heels.

The school is located in the heart of the basketball-rich ACC. Four of the conference's schools are in North Carolina.

Tar Heels fans enjoy spirited rivalries with North Carolina State and Wake Forest. But the North Carolina–Duke rivalry has long been one of college basketball's most heated.

North Carolina's first championship came in 1957. That year, coach Frank McGuire led the team to a 32–0 record.

Tar Heels freshman guard Michael Jordan lets go of the game-winning shot in the 1982 NCAA title game against Georgetown.

The Tar Heels capped the perfect season with a pair of thrilling triple-overtime wins on consecutive nights. The second one came in the NCAA title game, where the Tar Heels held off superstar Wilt Chamberlain and Kansas 54–53.

However, North Carolina's identity as a basketball power was largely established under coach Dean Smith. Upon his arrival in 1961–62, Smith built a culture of unselfish basketball called "The Carolina Way." After going 8–9 in his first year, Smith never had another losing record.

Smith delivered a second national title in 1982. With 15 seconds left in the title game against Georgetown, freshman Michael Jordan hit a jump shot to win the game 63–62. Smith's Tar Heels topped Michigan 77–71 in the 1993 championship. Smith retired four years later as the sport's all-time winningest coach. The school's arena is now named for the longtime coach.

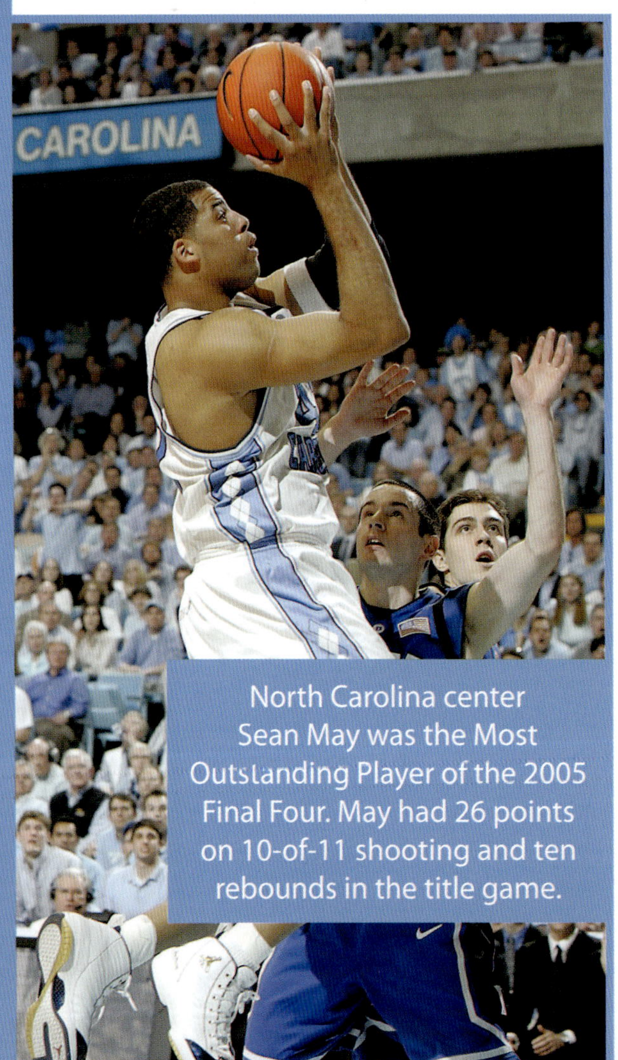

North Carolina center Sean May was the Most Outstanding Player of the 2005 Final Four. May had 26 points on 10-of-11 shooting and ten rebounds in the title game.

FACT BOX

First Season: 1910–11

Location: Chapel Hill, North Carolina

Arena: Dean E. Smith Center

Conference: Atlantic Coast Conference

All-Time Record: 2,395–874

NCAA Tournament Appearances: 54

Final Fours: 21

National Titles: 1957, 1982, 1993, 2005, 2009, 2017

Top Coaches: Frank McGuire (1952–61); Dean Smith (1961–97); Roy Williams (2003–21)

Top Players: Lennie Rosenbluth (1954–57); Charlie Scott (1967–70); Phil Ford (1974–78); James Worthy (1979–82); Michael Jordan (1981–84); Antawn Jamison (1995–98); Tyler Hansbrough (2005–09); RJ Davis (2020–25)

Mascot: Rameses

RUSHING FRANKLIN STREET

North Carolina students sprint through campus after big victories. They race to the intersection of Franklin and North Columbia streets to cheer together. Some celebrations grow incredibly large. An estimated 55,000 fans showed up at the intersection after North Carolina beat Gonzaga for the 2017 NCAA championship.

North Carolina's 37-year streak of winning seasons ended in 2001–02. After missing out on the tournament again the next year, the school hired former Smith assistant Roy Williams away from Kansas. Within two years, Williams had a dominant North Carolina team back on top. The Tar Heels went 33–4 and knocked off Illinois 75–70 for a fourth title in 2005. Williams led the team to championships again in 2009 and 2017 before retiring in 2021.

NORTH CAROLINA STATE WOLFPACK

The Wolfpack are often overshadowed by their two powerful neighbors, Duke and North Carolina. The ACC schools are all within 25 miles (40 km) of one another in the Raleigh-Durham "Triangle." And while Duke and North Carolina have had more success historically, the Wolfpack have a proud tradition too.

The team often called NC State has authored two of college basketball's most memorable upsets. In 1974, the Wolfpack were 28–1 entering the Final Four. The opposing UCLA Bruins were 26–4 and had won the previous seven national championships. UCLA had also been the only team to beat the Wolfpack that season.

In the rematch, high-flying NC State guard David Thompson led the

Guard David Thompson, *right*, scored 2,309 points at NC State from 1972 to 1975, a record that stood until 1991.

Coach Jim Valvano celebrates with his players after NC State upset Houston in the 1983 NCAA title game.

way with 28 points and ten rebounds. The Wolfpack held on to win 80–77 in double overtime. Thompson added 21 more points two days later against Marquette. NC State took home its first national championship with a 76–64 win.

In 1983, NC State entered the NCAA Tournament as a No. 6 seed. After surviving

THE V FOUNDATION

Popular NC State coach Jim Valvano died of cancer in 1993. Before his death, he created the V Foundation for Cancer Research. Since then, the foundation has raised more than $350 million. Some of that funding comes from the Jimmy V Classic, a tournament held each December in New York City.

one-possession wins against Pepperdine, UNLV, and No. 1 seed Virginia, the Wolfpack reached the championship game. There they faced heavily favored Houston. Many thought the fast-paced Cougars would blow away NC State.

At the time, the NCAA did not have a shot clock. To counter Houston's speed, Wolfpack coach Jim Valvano slowed the game down by stressing long possessions for his team. In the final seconds, the game was tied 52–52. NC State had the ball for a final shot. But after a fumbled pass, guard Dereck Whittenburg had to throw up a desperation shot from

NC State forward D. J. Burns scored a team-high 29 points in the Wolfpack's 76–64 upset of rival Duke in the 2024 Elite Eight.

nearly half-court. Whittenburg's shot fell short. But forward Lorenzo Charles was under the basket. He grabbed the miss and dunked home the winning basket as time expired. The energetic Valvano sprinted around the court after the basket in one of the NCAA Tournament's most memorable celebrations.

NC State nearly made another underdog championship run in the 2024 NCAA Tournament. The No. 11–seeded Wolfpack upset No. 6 Texas Tech, No. 2 Marquette, and No. 4 Duke to reach the Final Four. Their run finally ended with a 63–50 loss to No. 1 seed Purdue in the national semifinal.

FACT BOX

First Season: 1910–11

Location: Raleigh, North Carolina

Arena: Lenovo Center

Conference: Atlantic Coast Conference

All-Time Record: 1,828–1,155

NCAA Tournament Appearances: 27

Final Fours: 4

National Titles: 1974, 1983

Top Coaches: Everett Case (1946–65); Norm Sloan (1966–80); Jim Valvano (1980–90)

Top Players: Sam Ranzino (1947–51); Ronnie Shavlik (1953–56); Tom Burleson (1971–74); David Thompson (1972–75); Hawkeye Whitney (1976–80); Sidney Lowe (1979–83); Rodney Monroe (1987–91); Julius Hodge (2001–05)

Mascot: Mr. and Ms. Wuf

OHIO STATE BUCKEYES

Ohio State's John Schick (in white) goes up for a shot against Oregon in the first NCAA championship game in 1939.

Ohio State began playing basketball in 1898. But the program didn't take off until coach Harold Olsen arrived in 1922. The influential coach helped build the program into a Big Ten power.

Olsen was also a major force behind the creation of the first NCAA Tournament in 1939. After pushing for years for the tournament, Olsen and the Buckeyes advanced to the first-ever final. There, they fell 46–33 to Oregon.

Olsen left the team in 1946 after leading Ohio State to three more Final Fours. By the time coach Fred Taylor arrived in 1958, the Buckeyes had missed the NCAA Tournament eight years in a row. But two future superstars soon helped change that. After going 11–11 in Taylor's first season, the Buckeyes exploded to

25–3 in 1959–60. Behind center Jerry Lucas and forward John Havlicek, both sophomores, Ohio State returned to the NCAA final to face defending champion California. All five of Ohio State's starters scored in double figures. But Final Four Most Outstanding Player Lucas led the way with 16 points and ten rebounds. Ohio State buried California early, taking a 37–19 halftime lead on its way to a 75–55 win.

Over the next two seasons, Taylor's Buckeyes became the first team to play in three straight NCAA title games. But they fell in both the 1961 and 1962 finals to in-state rival Cincinnati. Taylor led one more Final Four charge in 1968. He left the team in 1976. Taylor's school record of 297 wins stood until Thad Matta broke it in 2015.

Ohio State didn't make it back to the Final Four until 1999. However, that appearance was later wiped out when it was discovered that Ohio State boosters were illegally paying players. The team was forced to void 94 wins between 1998 and 2002.

Buckeyes center Jerry Lucas earned All-America honors for the third time in three seasons in 1961–62.

Ohio State guard Evan Turner won the AP Player of the Year, the Naismith Award, and the Wooden Award in 2010.

In the wake of the scandal, Ohio State hired Matta. He led the Buckeyes back to the championship game in 2007 before losing to Florida. Five years later, the Buckeyes were back in the Final Four. They led most of the national semifinal against Kansas. However, Ohio State stumbled down the stretch and lost 64–62.

FACT BOX

First Season: 1898–99

Location: Columbus, Ohio

Arena: Value City Arena

Conference: Big Ten Conference

All-Time Record: 1,807–1,163

NCAA Tournament Appearances: 30

Final Fours: 10

National Titles: 1960

Top Coaches: Harold Olsen (1922–46); Fred Taylor (1958–76); Thad Matta (2004–17)

Top Players: Jerry Lucas (1959–62); John Havlicek (1959–62); Gary Bradds (1961–64); Herb Williams (1977–81); Dennis Hopson (1983–87); Jim Jackson (1989–92); Evan Turner (2007–10); Jared Sullinger (2010–12)

Mascot: Brutus Buckeye

COACH ON THE BENCH

One of Fred Taylor's bench players on the 1960 championship team was Bobby Knight. Knight averaged only 3.8 points per game in his career. But many teammates assumed he would make a great coach eventually because of the way he thought about the game. Knight ended up winning a then-record 899 games as a head coach at Army, Indiana, and Texas Tech. While at Indiana, Knight had a 40–18 career record against Ohio State.

OKLAHOMA SOONERS

Oklahoma's basketball success is often overlooked because of the team's incredible football history. But the Sooners have had many excellent basketball seasons as well. Oklahoma reached the very first Final Four in 1939. Coach Bruce Drake's team lost to eventual champion Oregon in the semifinals. But in 1947, All-America

Coach Billy Tubbs was known for his passionate coaching style during his 14 seasons at Oklahoma from 1980 to 1994.

TOP DAUG

Billy Tubbs borrowed the Oklahoma wrestling team's "Underdog" mascot when he took over the struggling basketball team in 1980. After Oklahoma became winners, "Underdog" became "Top Daug." The Top Daug mascot was known for wild antics during games, such as rappelling from the overhead scoreboard or bothering officials and opposing coaches. The mascot was retired in 2004 but brought back in 2020.

center Gerry Tucker carried the Sooners to the final. The team had survived narrow tournament wins over Oregon State and Texas but lost to Holy Cross in the title game.

After decades of struggling, the Sooners hired coach Billy Tubbs in 1980. The fiery coach soon revived the program. Tubbs played a high-tempo system that became known as "Billy Ball." In one 1989 game, the Sooners set an NCAA record by scoring 97 points in one half.

Explosive Sooners forward Blake Griffin averaged 22.7 points per game in 2008–09. He also led the nation averaging 14.4 rebounds per game.

Tubbs's most accomplished team took the floor in 1987–88. Smooth point guard Mookie Blaylock and powerful center Stacey King guided the Sooners to a 30–3 record, including winning the Big 8 Conference tournament. The No. 1 seed Sooners then reached the NCAA Tournament final against conference rival Kansas. The Sooners had beaten the

Jayhawks twice during the regular season but lost 83–79 in the third meeting.

Tubbs left in 1994. Under coach Kelvin Sampson, the Sooners reached the NCAA Tournament 11 times in the next 12 seasons. That included a run to the 2002 Final Four.

Some electrifying players have shined at Oklahoma in the years since then. Forward Blake Griffin's rim-rocking dunks helped him earn the Naismith Award as the nation's best player in 2008–09. In 2015–16, guard Buddy Hield dazzled fans with his long-distance shooting. He earned the Naismith Award after averaging 25.0 points per game. Hield also shot the Sooners into their fifth Final Four that season. In 2017–18, point guard Trae Young led the nation in both points and assists during his one season in Norman.

FACT BOX

First Season: 1907–08

Location: Norman, Oklahoma

Arena: Lloyd Noble Center

Conference: Southeastern Conference

All-Time Record: 1,796–1,163

NCAA Tournament Appearances: 34

Final Fours: 5

National Titles: None

Top Coaches: Bruce Drake (1938–55); Billy Tubbs (1980–94); Kelvin Sampson (1994–2006)

Top Players: Alvan Adams (1972–75); Wayman Tisdale (1982–85); Tim McCalister (1984–87); Stacey King (1985–89); Mookie Blaylock (1987–89); Jeff Webster (1989–94); Blake Griffin (2007–09); Buddy Hield (2012–16)

Mascot: Boomer and Sooner

Oklahoma guard Trae Young shoots over a defender during a 2018 game against Kansas State.

OKLAHOMA STATE COWBOYS

The Oklahoma State Cowboys were known as the Oklahoma A&M Aggies in the 1940s. During this decade, they became the NCAA Tournament's first dynasty. The Aggies were led by Hank Iba, who coached at the school for 36 years. Iba was a

Coach Hank Iba, *left*, won 654 games in 36 years at Oklahoma State before retiring in 1970.

shrewd coach who became known as "The Iron Duke of Defense" for his shutdown strategies. His most famous defensive innovation was known as "The Swinging Gate." In it, his players switched between man-to-man and zone defense as they moved around to cover the defensive zone.

In 1945, Iba and star center Bob Kurland led the Aggies to their first NCAA title. Kurland was 6 feet, 10 inches tall at a time when players that size were rare. He dominated inside. Kurland is widely thought to be the first college player ever to dunk in a game.

Center Bob Kurland was a three-time All-American at Oklahoma A&M during the 1940s.

Kurland scored 22 points in the 1945 NCAA championship game against New York University. Oklahoma A&M won 49–45. A year later, Kurland put up 23 points in the final against North Carolina. The Aggies escaped with a 43–40 victory to become the tournament's first repeat champions.

Iba coached the Cowboys until 1970. Many great coaches who came after him were influenced by Iba's success and wisdom. But the school that was renamed Oklahoma State in 1957 struggled to live up to his early success. Coach Eddie Sutton took over in 1990. One of Iba's former assistants, Sutton

NCAA VS. NIT

In the 1940s, the NIT was considered better than the NCAA Tournament. Two days after winning the 1945 NCAA Tournament, Oklahoma A&M took on NIT champion DePaul at Madison Square Garden in New York City. The game featured star big men Bob Kurland of Oklahoma A&M and George Mikan of DePaul. The Aggies won 52–44, proving that the NCAA champions were just as good as the NIT winners. The game also raised more than $50,000 for the American Red Cross.

Cowboys guard John Lucas III celebrates after his go-ahead shot in the final seconds of the 2004 Elite Eight.

FACT BOX

First Season: 1907–08

Location: Stillwater, Oklahoma

Arena: Gallagher-Iba Arena

Conference: Big 12 Conference

All-Time Record: 1,745–1,267

NCAA Tournament Appearances: 29

Final Fours: 6

National Titles: 1945, 1946

Top Coaches: Hank Iba (1934–70); Eddie Sutton (1990–2006); Travis Ford (2008–16)

Top Players: Bob Kurland (1942–46); Byron Houston (1988–92); Bryant Reeves (1991–95); Adrian Peterson (1995–99); Tony Allen (2002–04); Marcus Smart (2012–14); Phil Forte (2012–17); Cade Cunningham (2020–21)

Mascot: Pistol Pete

led a quick turnaround. In 1995, he led the team to the Final Four behind All-America center Bryant Reeves.

In 2001, the Cowboys were rocked by tragedy. A plane carrying members of the team's travel party crashed after a game. All ten on board died, including two players. Teammates of the deceased players were still on the Oklahoma State roster in 2004 when the team made its next deep NCAA Tournament run. With just under seven seconds left in the Elite Eight against Saint Joseph's, guard John Lucas III hit a three-point shot to win the game 64–62 and send the Cowboys to the Final Four for the sixth time. The next week, Oklahoma State's run ended with a 67–65 loss to Georgia Tech.

When Oregon reached the 2017 Final Four, the team brought the trophy won by the 1939 team to the tournament for inspiration.

Early on, most of college basketball's elite programs were from the eastern United States. However, Oregon often had strong teams throughout the early 1900s. Known at the time as the Webfoots, Oregon already had a winning program when Howard Hobson took over as coach in 1935.

Hobson stressed fast-paced basketball, which was rare for that era. His teams sped to 20 wins in each of his first four seasons, and in 1939 the Webfoots reached the first NCAA Tournament championship game. Though no Oregon player stood taller than 6 feet, 8 inches, the Webfoots still towered over other teams. A local sportswriter dubbed them "The Tall Firs" after the evergreen trees that grow all over the state.

In 1976, guard Ron Lee was the first Oregon player to reach 2,000 career points.

Led by 14 points from forward John Dick, Oregon easily beat Ohio State to become the first NCAA champion. Oregon didn't return to the tournament until 1945. In a season in which the Webfoots played an all-time record 45 games, Oregon lost to Arkansas 79–76 in the opening round.

It took Oregon decades to reach those heights again. In 2002, coach Ernie Kent led the team to

Ducks guard Tyler Dorsey cuts down the net after the 2017 Elite Eight. Dorsey had a team-high 27 points in the game.

HISTORY ON THE FLOOR

Oregon opened Matthew Knight Arena in January 2011. The court was designed to look like a ring of fir trees lining an open patch of sky. The unique design was a reference to Oregon's 1939 "Tall Firs" national championship team.

its first NCAA Tournament victory in 42 years. That season, the high-scoring Ducks fell to Kansas in the regional final.

Coach Dana Altman, who had taken over in 2010, led Oregon to a 33-win season in 2016–17. The Ducks entered the tournament as a

FACT BOX

First Season: 1902–03

Location: Eugene, Oregon

Arena: Matthew Knight Arena

Conference: Big Ten Conference

All-Time Record: 1,804–1,428

NCAA Tournament Appearances: 19

Final Fours: 2

National Titles: 1939

Top Coaches: Howard Hobson (1936–44, 1945–47); Ernie Kent (1997–2010); Dana Altman (2010–)

Top Players: Urgel Wintermute (1936–39); John Dick (1937–40); Ron Lee (1972–76); Anthony Taylor (1984–88); Luke Ridnour (2000–03); Luke Jackson (2000–04); Dillon Brooks (2014–17); Payton Pritchard (2016–20)

Mascot: The Oregon Duck

No. 3 seed. After close wins against Rhode Island and Michigan in the second and third rounds, Oregon routed Kansas 74–60 in the Elite Eight. That set up a Final Four matchup with North Carolina. The Ducks trailed 77–71 with a minute to go before rallying to within a point. North Carolina missed four free throws in the final ten seconds, but Oregon failed to grab the rebounds. The Ducks lost 77–76.

PRINCETON TIGERS

Forward Bill Bradley averaged 30.2 points per game at Princeton from 1962 to 1965.

Princeton has long been one of the top teams in the prestigious Ivy League. The conference is made up of many of the United States' top academic institutions. Its schools do not give out athletic scholarships. Despite those limits, the Tigers have stayed competitive on the court for decades.

Bill Bradley led Princeton's famous 1964–65 team. The 6-foot-5-inch forward was the only double-digit scorer on the roster. Behind him, the Tigers rolled to an Ivy League title. Bradley then scored 13 points in the final eight minutes of the opening round of the NCAA Tournament as the Tigers rallied to beat Penn State 60–58.

Bradley followed that performance with 27 points, 14 rebounds, and eight assists in a win over North Carolina State. In his next game, Bradley put up 41 points, ten rebounds, and nine assists in a 109–69 rout of Providence. That sent the

Tigers to the Final Four against Michigan. Despite 29 points from Bradley, the Wolverines knocked off the Tigers in the national semifinals. But Princeton's run wasn't over. At the time, the defeated semifinal teams played a third-place game. In the consolation championship, Bradley lit up Wichita State for a Final Four–record 58 points as Princeton won 118–82.

In 1967, Princeton hired Pete Carril as coach. Without superstars such as Bradley to lead the team, Carril developed a slowdown strategy. His players passed the ball patiently and deliberately, taking their time to work for an open layup. The complicated system of picks and cuts became known as "The Princeton Offense."

Princeton coach Pete Carril, *left*, speaks with CBS television after the Tigers upset UCLA in the 1996 NCAA Tournament. Carril retired after the season.

SENATOR BRADLEY

In addition to starring on the court, Bill Bradley was one of Princeton's most impressive students. He earned a prestigious Rhodes Scholarship to England's University of Oxford. Bradley later played ten years in the NBA, winning two titles. After his playing days, Bradley was elected to the US Senate representing New Jersey. Bradley served three Senate terms from 1979 to 1997. In 2000, he ran for president. Bradley lost in the Democratic primary to Al Gore.

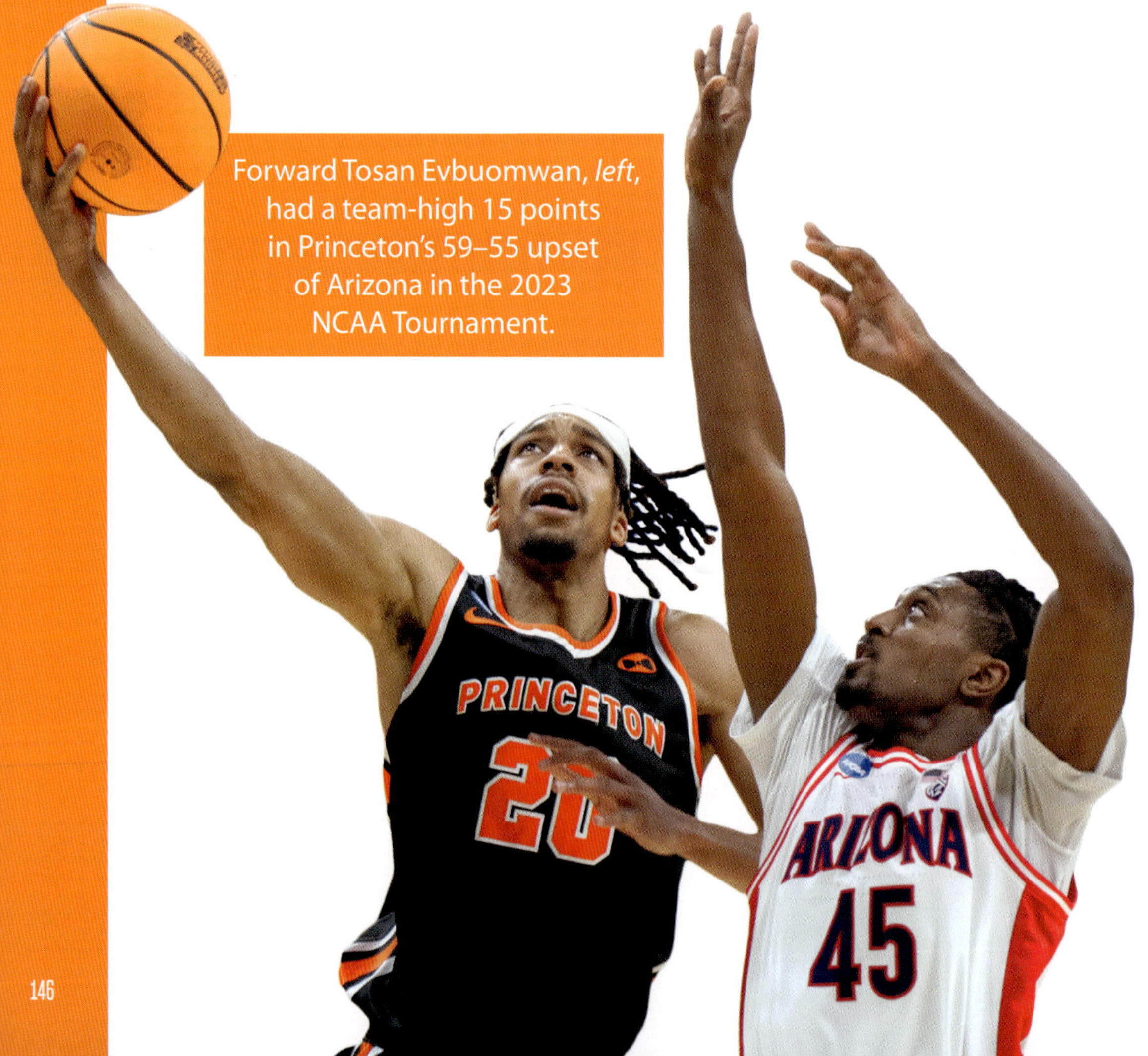

Forward Tosan Evbuomwan, *left*, had a team-high 15 points in Princeton's 59–55 upset of Arizona in the 2023 NCAA Tournament.

Carril's finest moment came in the opening round of the 1996 NCAA Tournament. The Tigers upset defending champion UCLA 43–41. Forward Gabe Lewullis scored the winning basket on a backdoor layup with four seconds left.

Mitch Henderson was a guard on the team that upset UCLA. In 2011, Henderson took over as Princeton's coach. In 2023, Henderson's No. 15–seeded Tigers upset Arizona and Missouri to reach the Sweet 16. It was Princeton's deepest tournament run since 1967, when the team also reached the regional semifinals.

FACT BOX

First Season: 1900–01

Location: Princeton, New Jersey

Arena: Jadwin Gymnasium

Conference: Ivy League

All-Time Record: 1,850–1,135

NCAA Tournament Appearances: 26

Final Fours: 1

National Titles: None

Top Coaches: Butch van Breda Kolff (1962–67); Pete Carril (1967–96); Mitch Henderson (2011–)

Top Players: Peter Campbell (1959–62); Bill Bradley (1962–65); Craig Robinson (1979–83); Kit Mueller (1987–91); Brian Earl (1995–99); Doug Davis (2008–12); Ian Hummer (2009–13); Devin Cannady (2015–19)

Mascot: The Tiger

PURDUE BOILERMAKERS

Purdue has established itself as one of the Big Ten's most successful programs, even as the Boilermakers continue to seek their first national championship. In 2024, Purdue won its 26th regular-season Big Ten title. That was four more than in-state rival Indiana, which sat in second place.

More than half of those titles came between 1911 and 1940. For much of that time, the Boilermakers were coached by Ward "Piggy" Lambert. The legendary coach played up-tempo basketball in an era when most teams slowed the game down. One of his best players was three-time All-America point guard John Wooden. The future iconic coach at UCLA led Purdue to a 17–1 record in 1931–32.

A statue of former Purdue star John Wooden sits outside the Boilermakers' Mackey Arena.

Forward Rick Mount, *right*, led the Big Ten in scoring in all three of his seasons at Purdue from 1967 to 1970.

Purdue fell short of more Big Ten glory between 1941 and 1968. But in the 1969 NCAA Tournament, high-scoring forward Rick Mount led the Boilermakers to the national championship game. Mount averaged 33.3 points per game. He had 28 in the final against Wooden's UCLA team. But Purdue lost 92–72.

In 1980, star center Joe Barry Carroll led Purdue to the Final Four. Once again, the Boilermakers were knocked out by UCLA. This time they fell in the national semifinals.

Purdue's tradition of dominant players continued into the 1990s and 2000s. The Naismith and Wooden awards are the nation's most prestigious national player of the year honors. In 1994, forward Glenn Robinson won both after averaging 30.3 points per game. Towering Purdue center Zach Edey matched that feat in 2023 and 2024. He became only the second man to win both awards in back-to-back years. In 2024, the 7-foot-4-inch Edey led the Boilermakers back to the NCAA title game. There, they were upended 75–60 by Connecticut.

Center Zach Edey became Purdue's all-time leading scorer in 2024. He finished with 2,516 points.

WHIFFING ON WOODEN

In 1947, Purdue offered John Wooden an assistant coaching job with the promise that he would become head coach in a few years. Wooden was uncomfortable with that arrangement and turned it down. Instead, he accepted the UCLA head job the following year. The Bruins went on to win ten national titles under Wooden in the 1960s and 1970s. He is recognized as one of the sport's all-time great coaches.

FACT BOX

First Season: 1896–97

Location: West Lafayette, Indiana

Arena: Mackey Arena

Conference: Big Ten Conference

All-Time Record: 1,953–1,092

NCAA Tournament Appearances: 35

Final Fours: 3

National Titles: None

Top Coaches: Piggy Lambert (1916–17, 1918–46); Gene Keady (1980–2005); Matt Painter (2005–)

Top Players: John Wooden (1929–32), Terry Dischinger (1959–62); Dave Schellhase (1963–66); Rick Mount (1967–70); Joe Barry Carroll (1976–80); Glenn Robinson (1992–94); E'Twaun Moore (2007–11); Zach Edey (2020–24)

Mascots: Boilermaker Special and Purdue Pete

SAINT JOHN'S RED STORM

Ray Wertis (4) of Saint John's goes up for a rebound against Manhattan College at New York City's Madison Square Garden in 1946.

New York City was the center of the basketball world in the first half of the 1900s. Saint John's was one of many great programs in the nation's largest city. In the two seasons between 1929 and 1931, coach James "Buck" Freeman's "Wonder Five" of Matty Begovich, Rip Gerson, Mac Kinsbrunner, Max Posnack, and Allie Schuckman led the team to a combined record of 44–2.

Saint John's reached its first NCAA championship game in 1952 under coach Frank McGuire. After an 80–63 loss to Kansas, McGuire shocked the college basketball world by leaving Saint John's for North Carolina. Many thought it was a step down for the coach. But he quickly turned the Tar Heels into a power. Saint John's remained a winning program, but the team reached only five of the next 23 NCAA Tournaments.

In the late 1970s, coach Lou Carnesecca built Saint John's back up by leaning on local New York talent. The school helped found the Big East Conference in 1979. Soon, Saint John's was at the heart of the most dominant college conference in the country. In 1985, the Big East became the first conference to send three teams to the Final Four in the same season. Saint John's, led by sharpshooting forward Chris Mullin, was one of them. But the Red Storm lost 77–59 to rival Georgetown in a highly anticipated national semifinal.

Lou Carnesecca often wore his trademark sweater while coaching at Saint John's from 1965 to 1970 and 1973 to 1992.

Carnesecca coached the Red Storm until 1992. After he left, Saint John's hired a series of high-profile coaches in an effort to keep the success going. However, many failed to keep the best local players in New York, despite the draw of playing many home games in the city's famous Madison Square Garden. Between 1992 and 2025, the Red Storm advanced past the second round of the NCAA Tournament only once.

New York City native Chris Mullin became Saint John's all-time leading scorer with 2,440 points in 1985. He later coached the Red Storm from 2015 to 2019.

FACT BOX

First Season: 1907–08

Location: Queens, New York

Arena: Carnesecca Arena/Madison Square Garden

Conference: Big East Conference

All-Time Record: 1,942–1,098

NCAA Tournament Appearances: 30

Final Fours: 2

National Titles: None

Top Coaches: James "Buck" Freeman (1927–36); Joe Lapchick (1936–47, 1956–65); Lou Carnesecca (1965–70, 1973–92)

Top Players: Dick McGuire (1943–44, 1946–49); Bob Zawoluk (1949–52); Chris Mullin (1981–85); Mark Jackson (1983–87); Malik Sealy (1988–92); Felipe Lopez (1994–98); D'Angelo Harrison (2011–15); RJ Luis Jr. (2023–25)

Mascot: Johnny Thunderbird

KINGS OF THE NIT

In the early days, Saint John's frequently turned down the NCAA Tournament to play in the higher-profile NIT. Saint John's won the tournament in 1943 and again in 1944. By the time the team won the NIT title again in 1959, the NCAA Tournament had passed the NIT in prestige. Saint John's added three more NIT titles in 1965, 1989, and 2003. Though the final title was later voided because of recruiting violations, Saint John's still led all schools with five official NIT championships as of 2025.

SYRACUSE ORANGE

Jim Boeheim retired after 47 years coaching Syracuse in 2023. Only two coaches in Division I men's basketball history spent more time at a school.

For most of its early history, Syracuse was a little-known team from central New York. But the Orange surged forward in the 1970s under coach Roy Danforth. In 1975, Danforth's undersized squad reached its first Final Four but lost to Kentucky in the national semifinals.

Jim Boeheim took over for Danforth before the 1976–77 season. Boeheim led the team into the Big East Conference three years later, and soon the Orange were regular contenders. Boeheim's teams were known for huge crowds at the 35,000-seat Carrier Dome, which was later renamed the JMA Wireless Dome. The Orange played a signature 2–3 zone defense, which bottled up the lane and forced opponents to shoot long shots.

Behind the play of forward Derrick Coleman and guard Sherman Douglas, the Orange reached the national championship game in 1987. They were beaten 74–73 by Indiana on a last-second shot. Nine years later, electrifying forward John Wallace led Syracuse on a surprise run to the 1996 title game. But this time, a heavily favored Kentucky team knocked off the Orange 76–67.

Everything came together for Syracuse in 2002–03. Point guard Gerry McNamara and lanky forward Hakim Warrick were both on their way to the top of Syracuse's all-time scoring list. But high-scoring freshman forward Carmelo Anthony, in his only college season, was the team's biggest star. The three players carried the team in the title game against Kansas.

Forward Carmelo Anthony was the Most Outstanding Player of the 2003 Final Four. He was the first freshman to win the award since 1986.

Syracuse forward Hakim Warrick, *right*, blocks Kansas guard Michael Lee's potential game-tying three-pointer in the final seconds of the 2003 NCAA title game.

THE PEARL

Dwayne "Pearl" Washington was Syracuse's best player during the school's early years in the Big East. The flashy guard grew up honing his skills on the playgrounds of New York City. His electrifying dribbling and slick layups wowed crowds, leading to a large spike in attendance. Coach Jim Boeheim often credits Washington with making Syracuse a nationally known team. After Washington died in 2016, the team honored him by adding his No. 31 to the court.

McNamara hit six first-half three-pointers against the Jayhawks. Anthony led Syracuse with 20 points. But Warrick struggled offensively, scoring only six points. He also missed two late free throws that might have sealed the win. However, Warrick got redemption by blocking a three-point attempt by Kansas guard Michael Lee in the final seconds. The key play preserved an 81–78 win.

Boeheim took Syracuse to two more Final Fours, in 2013 and 2016. He retired in 2023 with 1,015 wins. He trailed only Duke's Mike Krzyzewski on the all-time list.

FACT BOX

First Season: 1900–01

Location: Syracuse, New York

Arena: JMA Wireless Dome

Conference: Atlantic Coast Conference

All-Time Record: 2,007–995

NCAA Tournament Appearances: 39

Final Fours: 6

National Titles: 2003

Top Coaches: Lew Andreas (1924–50); Roy Danforth (1968–76); Jim Boeheim (1976–2023)

Top Players: Pearl Washington (1983–86); Sherman Douglas (1985–89); Derrick Coleman (1986–90); Lawrence Moten (1991–95); John Wallace (1992–96); Hakim Warrick (2001–05); Carmelo Anthony (2002–03); Gerry McNamara (2003–06)

Mascot: Otto the Orange

UCLA BRUINS

UCLA put together one of the most dominant championship runs in American sports during the 1960s and 1970s. The dynasty began in 1964. In that year's national title game, the Bruins routed Duke 98–83 to cap a perfect 30–0 season. UCLA followed that with a 91–80 victory over Michigan in the 1965 title game. Star guard Gail Goodrich poured in 42 points.

After missing the NCAA Tournament in 1966, the Bruins bounced back in a big way. The team won every NCAA championship from 1967 to 1973. During that stretch, UCLA lost only five games.

The Bruins' run was fueled by two dominant big men. High-scoring 7-foot, 2-inch center Lew Alcindor,

Center Lew Alcindor averaged 26.4 points and 15.5 rebounds per game in three seasons at UCLA from 1966 to 1969.

UCLA coach John Wooden celebrates after winning his final NCAA championship in 1975.

who later changed his name to Kareem Abdul-Jabbar, was named the Most Outstanding Player of three straight Final Fours from 1967 to 1969. Soon after he left, Bill Walton took over in the middle. Walton averaged more than 20 points and 15 rebounds per game in his college career.

The constant of UCLA's incredible run was coach John Wooden. Known as "The Wizard of Westwood," he stressed

UCLA forward Ed O'Bannon (31) puts up a hook shot over Arkansas in the 1995 NCAA title game.

high-pressure, full-court defense. UCLA often won games by forcing opponents into mistakes. On offense, Wooden wanted good ball movement. He discouraged flashy play. Wooden often removed players from games if they dribbled between their legs.

Wooden added a final title in 1975 before retiring. The Wooden Award, named in his honor, is one of the main national player of the year awards. In 1995, UCLA forward Ed O'Bannon won the award while leading UCLA to its first title in two decades. He put up 30 points and 17 rebounds in an 89–78 win over Arkansas in the championship game.

THE STREAK

On January 30, 1971, UCLA beat UC–Santa Barbara 74–61. The Bruins didn't lose again until January 19, 1974. That afternoon, Notre Dame toppled UCLA in a thrilling 71–70 game. UCLA's streak lasted more than 1,000 days and covered 88 games. No other team in the history of men's college basketball has won more than 60 games in a row.

The Bruins remained NCAA Tournament regulars into the 2000s. Coach Ben Howland led them to three straight Final Fours from 2006 to 2008. The first of those teams reached the national title game but lost to Florida.

In 2021, coach Mick Cronin guided the team to another Final Four. And four years later, he ushered the team into a new era as a member of the Big Ten. Though the Bruins had added only one title over a span of 50 years, their 11 championships remained the most of any team.

FACT BOX

First Season: 1919–20

Location: Los Angeles, California

Arena: Pauley Pavilion

Conference: Big Ten Conference

All-Time Record: 2,025–916

NCAA Tournament Appearances: 51

Final Fours: 18

National Titles: 1964, 1965, 1967, 1968, 1969, 1970, 1971, 1972, 1973, 1975, 1995

Top Coaches: John Wooden (1948–75); Jim Harrick (1988–96); Ben Howland (2003–13)

Top Players: Walt Hazzard (1961–64); Gail Goodrich (1962–65); Lew Alcindor (1966–69); Sidney Wicks (1968–71); Bill Walton (1971–74); Jamaal "Keith" Wilkes (1971–74); Marques Johnson (1973–77); Reggie Miller (1983–87); Ed O'Bannon (1991–95)

Mascots: Joe and Josephine "Josie" Bruin

UNLV RUNNIN' REBELS

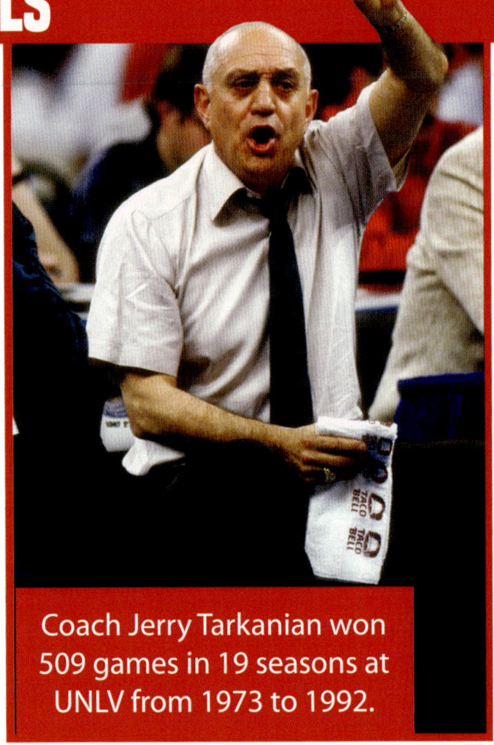

Coach Jerry Tarkanian won 509 games in 19 seasons at UNLV from 1973 to 1992.

When the University of Nevada, Las Vegas (UNLV) first joined Division I in 1969, few people knew much about the team. The school was often jokingly called "Tumbleweed Tech" because of its remote desert location. But UNLV quickly became a prominent team after coach Jerry Tarkanian was hired in 1973.

Tarkanian's teams lived up to UNLV's Runnin' Rebels nickname. His teams played at a fast pace and pressured opponents on defense. That showed in 1976–77, when UNLV averaged 107.1 points per game and advanced to its first Final Four.

TARK'S TOWEL

UNLV coach Jerry Tarkanian regularly manned the sideline with a towel draped over his shoulder. Often, he was spotted chewing on his towel. He began doing so early in his coaching career to prevent his mouth from becoming dry. But it became one of the popular coach's most famous quirks. UNLV erected a statue of Tarkanian outside the Thomas & Mack Center in 2013. It shows the famous coach sitting on the bench chewing on a towel.

UNLV fans loved Tarkanian. However, the coach frequently ran afoul of NCAA rules. The Runnin' Rebels were put on probation five months after their first Final Four appearance. The team had to sit out of postseason play for two years.

Tarkanian and the Runnin' Rebels bounced back and reached the Final Four again in 1987. By then, the NCAA was investigating UNLV for recruiting violations. Despite the distractions, UNLV emerged as a dominant force in 1989–90. Behind versatile forward Larry Johnson, the Runnin' Rebels went 35–5. In the NCAA Tournament, UNLV won three of its six games by 30-point margins. That included a 103–73 rout of Duke in the national title game. It was the largest margin

UNLV's Moses Scurry, *left*, and Anderson Hunt hug coach Jerry Tarkanian near the end of the 1990 NCAA title game victory over Duke.

UNLV forward Larry Johnson won both the Naismith Award and the Wooden Award in 1991.

of victory in NCAA championship-game history. Johnson had 22 points, while guard Anderson Hunt led all scorers with 29.

Many expected UNLV to repeat in 1991 when the team rolled into the Final Four 34–0. Instead, the Runnin' Rebels were upset by Duke 79–77. Within two years, UNLV was on probation again. Though fans protested, Tarkanian was let go. In the following three decades, UNLV made only eight NCAA Tournament appearances. Their deepest run was to the Sweet 16 in 2006–07.

FACT BOX

First Season: 1958–59

Location: Las Vegas, Nevada

Arena: Thomas & Mack Center

Conference: Mountain West Conference

All-Time Record: 1,205–562*

NCAA Tournament Appearances: 20

Final Fours: 4

National Titles: 1990

Top Coaches: Jerry Tarkanian (1973–92); Lon Kruger (2004–11); Dave Rice (2011–16)

Top Players: Eddie Owens (1973–77); Reggie Theus (1975–78); Sidney Green (1979–83); Freddie Banks (1983–87); Armen Gilliam (1984–87); Stacey Augmon (1987–91); Greg Anthony (1988–91); Larry Johnson (1989–91)

Mascot: Hey Reb!

** Since joining Division I in 1969–70*

Forward Paul Arizin, *right*, was named Villanova's first All-American in 1950.

Located near basketball-rich Philadelphia, Villanova has long been at the heart of college basketball. The Wildcats competed in the first Final Four in 1939 but lost in the semifinals. Despite decades of winning, Villanova didn't get back to the Final Four until 1971. Even the play of Final Four Most Outstanding Player Howard Porter couldn't carry the Wildcats past a dominant UCLA team, however. And the Final Four appearance was later removed from the record books when Porter was ruled ineligible.

Villanova helped form the Big East Conference in 1979. In the conference's early days, the Wildcats often looked up at dominant teams such as Syracuse, St. John's, and Georgetown. That changed in 1985. Villanova reached the NCAA Tournament as a No. 8 seed. The Wildcats then went on a thrilling run to the title game. Coach Rollie Massimino's team wasn't given much of a chance against rival Georgetown and its dominant center, Patrick Ewing. The Wildcats shocked the basketball world by playing a nearly perfect game. Villanova made 79 percent of its shots and came away with a 66–64 upset win.

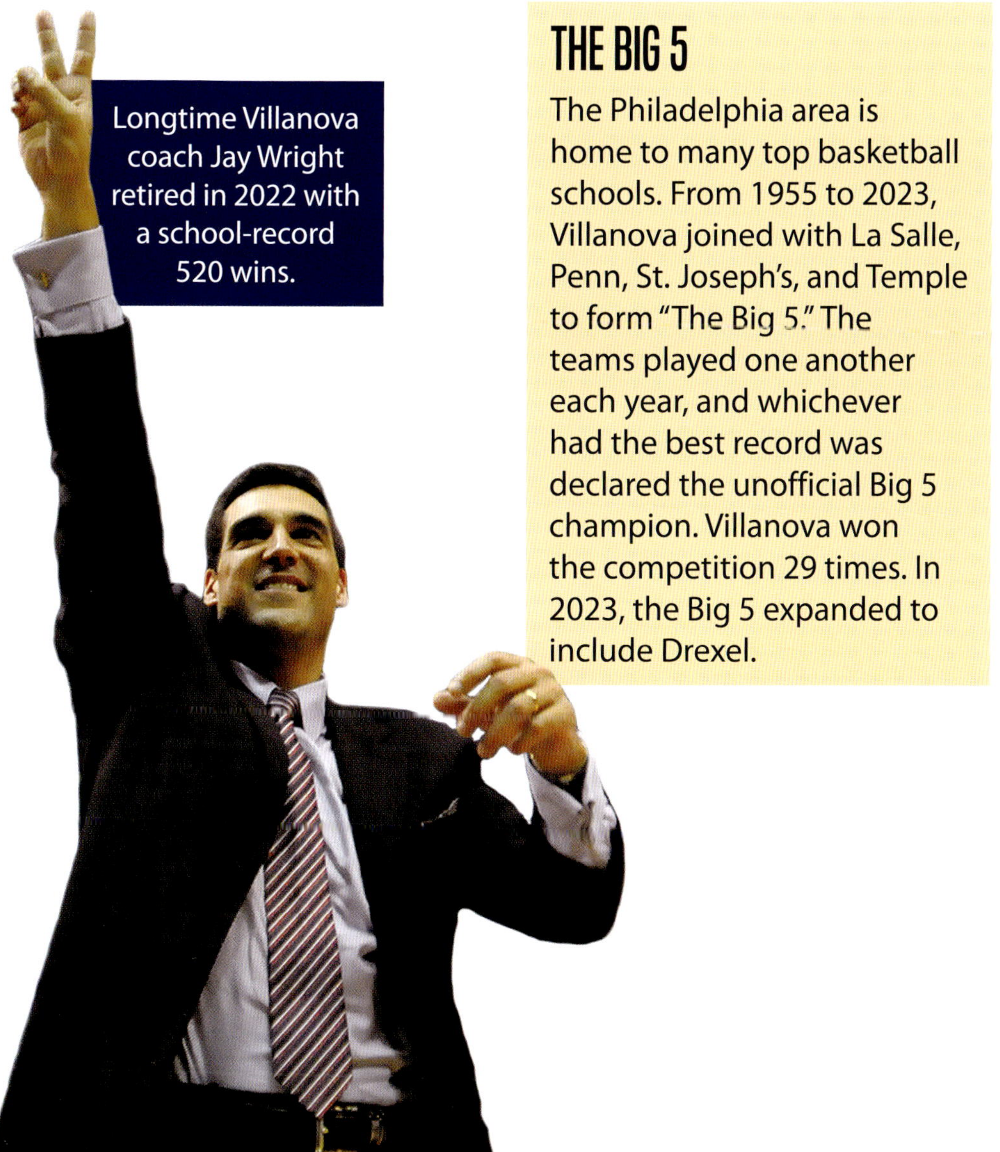

Longtime Villanova coach Jay Wright retired in 2022 with a school-record 520 wins.

THE BIG 5

The Philadelphia area is home to many top basketball schools. From 1955 to 2023, Villanova joined with La Salle, Penn, St. Joseph's, and Temple to form "The Big 5." The teams played one another each year, and whichever had the best record was declared the unofficial Big 5 champion. Villanova won the competition 29 times. In 2023, the Big 5 expanded to include Drexel.

Villanova forward Kris Jenkins lets go of his title-winning shot in the 2016 NCAA championship game against North Carolina.

The Wildcats couldn't match that glorious season until three decades later. In 2016, coach Jay Wright's team met North Carolina in the championship game. The Tar Heels tied the game 74–74 with 4.6 seconds left on an off-balance, desperation three-pointer. Then, at the final buzzer, Villanova forward Kris Jenkins broke the tie with a leaning three-pointer. It was the first time since 1963 that the title game ended on a shot as time expired.

Two years later, Wright's Wildcats were dominant. Behind guard Jalen Brunson and forward Mikal Bridges, Villanova led the nation with 86.6 points per game. In the NCAA Tournament, the Wildcats won each of their first five games by at least 12 points. The hot streak continued for the 35–4 Wildcats in the national title game. They blew out Michigan 79–62 to claim the program's third national championship.

FACT BOX

First Season: 1920–21

Location: Villanova, Pennsylvania

Arena: William B. Finneran Pavilion/Wells Fargo Center

Conference: Big East Conference

All-Time Record: 1,903–1,004

NCAA Tournament Appearances: 40

Final Fours: 6

National Titles: 1985, 2016, 2018

Top Coaches: Alex Severance (1936–61); Rollie Massimino (1973–92); Jay Wright (2001–22)

Top Players: Paul Arizin (1947–50); Howard Porter (1968–71); Kerry Kittles (1992–96); Randy Foye (2002–06); Scottie Reynolds (2006–10); Josh Hart (2013–17); Jalen Brunson (2015–18); Eric Dixon (2020–25)

Mascot: Will D. Cat

VIRGINIA CAVALIERS

Virginia emerged as a strong program in the new Southern Conference under coach Henry "Pop" Lannigan in the 1920s. But by the time the Cavaliers helped found the ACC in 1953, Virginia was a struggling team. That did not change until the mid-1970s when coach Terry Holland arrived. Known as a gentlemanly coach, Holland led Virginia through the 1980s. Behind superstar 7-foot, 4-inch center Ralph Sampson, the Cavaliers reached the Final Four in 1981. They did so again in 1984.

Virginia center Ralph Sampson dominated college basketball during the early 1980s.

Virginia later fell out of the nation's elite until coach Tony Bennett took over in 2009. Using an approach that combined patient offense with stifling defense, his Cavaliers were often one of the top-rated defensive teams in the country. In 2018, they appeared ready to deliver a championship. Instead, top-seeded Virginia was shocked by No. 16 seed Maryland–Baltimore County in the first round. The Cavaliers became the first men's No. 1 seed ever to fall to a No. 16 seed.

Tony Bennett, *right*, had only one losing season in 15 years coaching Virginia from 2009 to 2024.

Virginia bounced back the next season and reached the Final Four with a 33–3 record. The Cavaliers' run appeared to be over when they trailed Auburn by 10 in the final five minutes of the national semifinals. But they rallied back. With 0.6 seconds remaining, Virginia guard Kyle Guy was fouled on a three-pointer. He sank all three shots to seal a 63–62 victory.

Virginia and Texas Tech met in the championship game. After the teams battled to a 68–68 tie in regulation, the Cavaliers broke out for 17 points in the

SAMPSON IS GOLIATH

Ralph Sampson was one of the most dominant college players in history. In his four college seasons, the towering center averaged 16.9 points per game. He also led the ACC in rebounding three times. In his freshman season of 1979–80, Sampson averaged a national-best 4.6 blocks per game. Sampson won the Naismith Award in 1981, 1982, and 1983. Four decades later, he was still the award's only three-time winner.

five-minute overtime period. Guy was named the Final Four's Most Outstanding Player after pouring in 24 points in the final. But teammate De'Andre Hunter scored a game-high 27 points.

FACT BOX

First Season: 1905–06

Location: Charlottesville, Virginia

Arena: John Paul Jones Arena

Conference: Atlantic Coast Conference

All-Time Record: 1,757–1,232

NCAA Tournament Appearances: 26

Final Fours: 3

National Titles: 2019

Top Coaches: Henry Lannigan (1905–29); Terry Holland (1974–90); Tony Bennett (2009–24)

Top Players: Buzzy Wilkinson (1952–55); Barry Parkhill (1970–73); Wally Walker (1972–76); Jeff Lamp (1977–81); Ralph Sampson (1979–83); Bryant Stith (1988–92); Sean Singletary (2004–08); Malcolm Brogdon (2011–16)

Mascot: Cavman

The Cavaliers celebrate after defeating Texas Tech in the 2019 NCAA championship game.

The guard's biggest basket was a three-pointer with 2:10 left to put Virginia up. The Cavaliers pulled away for an 85–77 win and the school's first national title.

WEST VIRGINIA MOUNTAINEERS

West Virginia first achieved basketball success in 1942. That year, the Mountaineers took part in the NIT. At the time, that was considered more prestigious than the NCAA Tournament. After knocking off favored Long Island in the first round, West Virginia dominated Toledo 51–39 in the semifinals. The Mountaineers then outlasted Western Kentucky 47–45 in the championship game.

West Virginia guard Rod Hundley was named an All-American in 1956–57.

In the 1950s, two local stars helped raise the profile of the team. Guard Rod Hundley was a native of Charleston, West Virginia. In three seasons, he scored 2,180 points. His crafty dribbling earned him the nickname "Hot Rod."

After Hundley graduated, Jerry West of Chelyan, West Virginia, joined the team. The well-rounded guard broke Hundley's scoring record. He also led West Virginia to the 1959 NCAA title game. California beat West Virginia 71–70 to lift the trophy. But West was still named the Final Four's Most Outstanding Player. He scored at least 28 points and grabbed 11 or more rebounds in all five of the Mountaineers' tournament games.

West Virginia didn't reach those heights again until 2007. Coach John Beilein led the team to

West Virginia put up a statue of guard Jerry West, the 1959 Final Four Most Outstanding Player, outside its home arena in 2007.

INFLUENCERS

Two of West Virginia's best players became powerful figures in the world of professional basketball. Jerry West starred for the Los Angeles Lakers before becoming a successful general manager. His likeness still lives on in the NBA logo. Rod Thorn played for West Virginia from 1960 to 1963. He later became the NBA's vice president of operations. He also led the selection committee for the 1992 US Olympic men's basketball team that was the first to use professional players. Thorn's "Dream Team" dominated the Olympic Games in Barcelona, Spain.

Mountaineers forward Da'Sean Butler tries to split three Kentucky defenders for a shot in the 2010 Elite Eight.

a second NIT title before leaving for Michigan. In his place, West Virginia hired former Cincinnati coach Bob Huggins. In 2009–10, Huggins led an aggressive Mountaineers team to a 31–7 record. The No. 2–seeded Mountaineers then knocked off No. 1 seed Kentucky 73–66 in the Elite Eight. However, the run came to an end against eventual-champion Duke in the Final Four.

FACT BOX

First Season: 1903–04

Location: Morgantown, West Virginia

Arena: WVU Coliseum

Conference: Big 12 Conference

All-Time Record: 1,874–1,188

NCAA Tournament Appearances: 31

Final Fours: 2

National Titles: 0

Top Coaches: Fred Schaus (1954–60); Gale Catlett (1978–2002); Bob Huggins (2007–23)

Top Players: Scotty Hamilton (1940–43); Hot Rod Hundley (1954–57); Jerry West (1957–60); Rod Thorn (1960–63); Da'Sean Butler (2006–10); Jevon Carter (2014–18)

Mascot: WVU Mountaineer

WISCONSIN BADGERS

In 1940–41, Wisconsin started its season by losing three of its first eight games. But coach Bud Foster's Badgers turned things around. The team won its final 12 regular-season games and then three more in the NCAA Tournament. Led by star John Kotz, Wisconsin knocked off Washington State in the final to

Wisconsin guard Mike Kelley led the Big Ten with 2.6 steals per game in 1999–2000.

clinch the Badgers' first national championship.

The team's victory did not lead to more success, however. Wisconsin played in the NCAA Tournament only once in the next 52 years. But Wisconsin started a gradual turnaround in the late 1990s. Using his trademark slowdown style, coach Dick Bennett turned Wisconsin into a top defensive team.

Coach Bo Ryan holds up the trophy after Wisconsin beat Illinois 70–53 to win the 2004 Big Ten Tournament.

In 2000, the No. 8 seed Badgers made a surprise NCAA Tournament run. They upset No. 1 seed Arizona 66–59 in the second round. Wisconsin reached the Final Four but lost to Big Ten rival Michigan State in the national semifinals.

Bennett turned the program over to Bo Ryan in 2001. Ryan reached the NCAA Tournament in each of his 14 full seasons as coach. In that stretch, the Badgers won their first-round game 13 times. The team's high point came in the mid-2010s. The Badgers reached the Final Four for a third time in 2014 behind strong performances from center Frank Kaminsky and forward

Sam Dekker. Kaminsky scored six of Wisconsin's 10 overtime points in a 64–63 Elite Eight victory over Arizona. However, the Badgers once again fell in the national semifinals, this time to Kentucky.

In 2015, Kaminsky earned the Naismith Award as the nation's top player. The No. 1 seed Badgers again faced Arizona in the Elite Eight. Wisconsin won 85–78 behind 29 points from Kaminsky and 27 from Dekker. Kaminsky then added 20 points and 11 rebounds in a 71–64 win over Kentucky to reach the

Badgers center Frank Kaminsky (44) blocks a shot against Kentucky in the 2015 Final Four.

title game. However, the Badgers were upended by Duke, 68–63. Longtime assistant Greg Gard took over as coach when Ryan retired in December 2015. He led the Badgers to seven NCAA Tournaments in his first ten seasons.

WORTH THE WAIT

Wisconsin's 20 Big Ten titles through 2025 were the fourth-most of any conference team. But the Badgers had a big gap between titles. Wisconsin won the conference 14 times between 1907 and 1947. The Badgers didn't win again until 2002.

FACT BOX

First Season: 1898–99

Location: Madison, Wisconsin

Arena: Kohl Center

Conference: Big Ten Conference

All-Time Record: 1,732–1,299

NCAA Tournament Appearances: 28

Final Fours: 4

National Titles: 1941

Top Coaches: Bud Foster (1934–59); Bo Ryan (2001–15); Greg Gard (2015–)

Top Players: John Kotz (1940–43); Ab Nicholas (1949–52); Michael Finley (1991–95); Alando Tucker (2002–07); Jordan Taylor (2008–12); Frank Kaminsky (2011–15); Nigel Hayes (2013–17); Ethan Happ (2015–19)

Mascot: Bucky Badger

ALL-TIME NCAA RECORDS

CAREER RECORDS

Points
Pete Maravich, LSU (1967–70): 3,667

Rebounds
Tom Gola, La Salle (1951–55): 2,201

Assists
Bobby Hurley, Duke (1989–93): 1,076

Steals
Jacob Gilyard, Richmond (2019–22): 466

Blocks
Jarvis Varnado, Mississippi State (2006–10): 564

Three-Pointers Made
Antoine Davis, Detroit Mercy (2018–23): 588

Free-Throw Percentage
Blake Ahearn, Missouri State (2003–07): 94.6 percent

SINGLE-SEASON RECORDS

Points
Pete Maravich, LSU (1969–70): 1,381

Rebounds
Walt Dukes, Seton Hall (1952–53): 734

Assists
Mark Wade, UNLV (1986–87): 406

Steals
Desmond Cambridge, Alabama A&M (2001–02): 160

Blocks
David Robinson, Navy (1985–86): 207

LSU
23

DAVIDSON
30

Three-Pointers Made

Stephen Curry, Davidson (2007–08): 162
Darius McGhee, Liberty (2022–23): 162

Free-Throw Percentage

Blake Ahearn, Missouri State (2003–04): 97.1 percent

SINGLE-GAME RECORDS

Points

Frank Selvy, Furman (February 13, 1954): 100

Rebounds

Bill Chambers, William & Mary (February 14, 1953): 51

Assists

Cameron Parker, Sacred Heart (December 1, 2019): 24

Steals

Mookie Blaylock, Oklahoma (December 12, 1987, and December 17, 1988): 13
Nelson Phillips, Troy (November 23, 2022): 13

Blocks

Mickell Gladness, Alabama A&M (February 24, 2007): 16

Three-Pointers Made

Keith Veney, Marshall (December 14, 1996): 15
Josh Williams, Robert Morris (November 14, 2018): 15
Jordan Lyons, Furman (November 15, 2018): 15

Free Throws Made

Pete Maravich, LSU (December 22, 1969): 30
Ben Woodside, North Dakota State (December 12, 2008): 30

GLOSSARY

All-American

A player chosen as one of the best amateurs in the country in a particular sport.

blue blood

A historically prominent and successful program.

booster

Someone who enthusiastically supports a program, often by donating money.

Cinderella

In sports, a player or team that achieves much greater success than expected.

double-double

Accumulating ten or more of two certain statistics in a game.

dynasty

An extended period of excellence or success for a team.

overtime

An extra period of play when the score is tied after regulation.

poll

A survey of opinions on a subject, often used to rank college basketball teams during the season.

prestigious

Highly thought of.

probation

Being subject to strict rules and regulations as a punishment for breaking the rules.

recruiting

Persuading a high school player to attend a certain college, usually to play sports.

rival

An opponent with whom a player or team has a fierce and ongoing competition.

scholarship

Money provided to a student to pay for his or her education.

segregated

Separated based on race, gender, ethnicity, or other factors.

shot clock

A clock that counts down the number of seconds remaining before a basketball team must shoot the ball.

triple-double

Accumulating ten or more of three certain statistics in a game.

underdog

The person or team that is not expected to win.

upset

To unexpectedly beat a team that was heavily favored to win.

TO LEARN MORE

FURTHER READINGS

Ellis, Abigail, ed. *Illustrated Sports Encyclopedia*. DK Penguin Random House, 2023.

Giedd, Steph. *Basketball Strategies*. Abdo, 2024.

Hanlon, Luke. *Everything Basketball*. Abdo, 2024.

ONLINE RESOURCES

To learn more about men's college basketball, please visit **abdobooklinks.com** or scan this QR code. These links are routinely monitored and updated to provide the most current information available.

INDEX

PHOTO CREDITS

Cover Photos: Shutterstock Images, front (hoop); Mitchell Layton/Getty Images Sport/Getty Images, front (Zach Edey); Alex Slitz/Getty Images Sport/Getty Images, front (Cooper Flagg); Allsport/Hulton Archive/Getty Images, front (Shaquille O'Neal); Bettmann/Getty Images, front (Lew Alcindor); Focus On Sport/Getty Images, front (Michael Jordan); Tom Pennington/Getty Images Sport/Getty Images, back (trophy); GBF/AP Images, back (Indiana team)

Interior Photos: David J. Phillip/AP Images, 1, 85; Jamie Schwaberow/NCAA Photos/Getty Images, 3, 18–19, 47; AP Images, 4, 5, 12–13, 75, 137, 160, 161, 177; Ed Maloney/AP Images, 6, 8; Anthony Camerano/AP Images, 7; UPI/Bettmann Archive/Getty Images, 9; Rich Clarkson/NCAA Photos/Getty Images, 10, 90–91, 91, 94, 98, 99, 110, 116, 118–119, 144, 185; Chuck Burton/AP Images, 14; Gregory Shamus/Getty Images Sport/Getty Images, 15, 186; Rogelio V. Solis/AP Images, 16; Michael Chang/Getty Images Sport/Getty Images, 20–21; Jeff Fishbein/Sporting News/Getty Images, 21; Ronald Martinez/Getty Images Sport/Getty Images, 22, 170; Peter G. Aiken/WireImage/Getty Images, 24; Bernstein Associates/Getty Images Sport/Getty Images, 25; Brian Bahr/Getty Images Sport/Getty Images, 26; Bettmann/Getty Images, 28, 40, 78–79, 83, 114, 121, 125, 136, 152, 168, 176; Doug Pensinger/Allsport/Getty Images Sport/Getty Images, 29, 54; Bob Jordan/AP Images, 30; Alex Slitz/Getty Images Sport/Getty Images, 32–33; Mark Humphrey/AP Images, 33, 80–81; John Autey/MediaNews Group/St. Paul Pioneer Press/Getty Images, 34; Jerry Larson/AP Images, 36; Rod Aydelotte/Waco Tribune Herald/AP Images, 37; Justin Casterline/Getty Images Sport/Getty Images, 38–39; Todd Warshaw/Allsport/Getty Images Sport/Getty Images, 41; Jamie Sabau/Getty Images Sport/Getty Images, 42; Mark J. Terrill/AP Images, 44; Ryan McKee/NCAA Photos/Getty Images, 45; Lance King/Getty Images Sport/Getty Images, 48; Streeter Lecka/Getty Images Sport/Getty Images, 49, 122; Ned Dishman/Getty Images Sport/Getty Images, 50; Charles Arbogast/AP Images, 52–53; Amy Sancetta/AP Images, 52–53; Andy Lyons/Getty Images Sport/Getty Images, 55, 82, 182; Sam Hodde/Getty Images Sport/Getty Images, 56–57; Doug Mills/AP Images, 58; Bill Kostroun/AP Images, 59; Ted Mathias/AP Images, 60; Michael Conroy/AP Images, 62; Jed Jacobsohn/Getty Images Sport/Getty Images, 63, 107; Andy Lyons/Getty Images Sport/Getty Images, 64; Sam Pierson Jr./Houston Chronicle/AP Images, 66; Richard Mackson/Sports Illustrated/Getty Images, 67; Jamie Squire/Getty Images Sport/Getty Images, 68, 103; Jonathan Daniel/Getty Images Sport/Getty Images, 70; Allsport/Hulton Archives/Getty Images, 71; M. Spencer Green/AP Images, 72; GBF/AP Images, 74; Tom Strickland/AP Images, 76; WPS/AP Images, 78; H. B. Littell/AP Images, 86; NCAA Photos/Getty Images, 87, 128; Phil Sears/Allsport/Getty Images Sport/Getty Images, 88; Tony Gutierrez/AP Images, 92; Brad Messina/Allsport/Hulton Archive/Getty Images, 95; Bob Leverone/Sporting News Archive/Getty Images, 96–97, 120–121; Charlie Neibergall/AP Images, 100; Focus On Sport/Getty Images, 102, 153, 164; Doug Pensinger/Getty Images Sport/Getty Images, 104, 138; Allsport/Getty Images Sport/Getty Images, 106, 108; Ed Reinke/AP Images, 111, 157; Albert Pena/Cal Sport Media/AP Images, 112; Dave Martin/AP Images, 114–115; James Drake/Sports Illustrated Classic/Getty Images, 119; Harold Valentine/AP Images, 124; Nicholas Faulkner/Icon Sportswire/Getty Images, 126; Harvey Eugene Smith/AP Images, 129; Andy Altenburger/Icon Sport Media/Icon Sportswire/Getty Images, 130; Mitchell Layton/Getty Images Sport/Getty Images, 132, 150–151; Alonzo Adams/AP Images, 133; Peter G. Aiken/Getty Images Sport/Getty Images, 135; Tom Pennington/Getty Images Sport/Getty Images, 140; Ray Stubblebine/AP Images, 141; Charlie Riedel/AP Images, 142–143; Jamie Squire/Allsport/Getty Images Sport/Getty Images, 145; José Luis Villegas/AP Images, 146; Michael Allio/Icon Sportswire/AP Images, 148; MM/AP Images, 149; Peter Morgan/AP Images, 154; Kevin Rivoli/AP Images, 156; Bill Haber/AP Images, 158; Stephen Dunn/Getty Images Sport/Getty Images, 162; Susan Ragan/AP Images, 165; Ken Levine/Getty Images Sport/Getty Images, 166; Michael Perez/AP Images, 169; Wally McNamee/Corbis Historical/Getty Images, 172; Joel Auerbach/Getty Images Sport/Getty Images, 173; Matt Marriott/NCAA Photos/Getty Images, 174–175; Jim McIsaac/Getty Images Sport/Getty Images, 178–179; Jonathan Daniel/Allsport/Getty Images Sport/Getty Images, 180; Elsa/Getty Images Sport/Getty Images, 181

ABDOBOOKS.COM

Published by Abdo Reference, a division of ABDO, PO Box 398166, Minneapolis, Minnesota 55439.

Printed in China.
102025
012026

Editor: Chrös McDougall
Series Designer: Colleen McLaren
Production Designer: Karli Hughes

LIBRARY OF CONGRESS CONTROL NUMBER: 2025939307

PUBLISHER'S CATALOGING-IN-PUBLICATION DATA

Names: Beattie, Charlie, author.
Title: The men's college basketball encyclopedia / by Charlie Beattie
Description: Minneapolis, Minnesota: Abdo Reference, 2026 | Series: College sports encyclopedias | Includes online resources and index.
Identifiers: ISBN 9781098298852 (lib. bdg.) | ISBN 9798384932659 (ebook)
Subjects: LCSH: Basketball--Juvenile literature. | College sports--Juvenile literature. | Basketball teams--Juvenile literature. | Basketball--Records--Juvenile literature. | Sports--United States--History--Juvenile literature. | Encyclopedias--Juvenile literature.
Classification: DDC 796.323--dc23